Martin Esslin was born in 1918 and educated at Vienna. He read English and Philosophy at Vienna University. From 1936 to 1938 he trained as a director at the Reinhardt Seminar of Dramatic Art in Vienna. He joined the BBC in 1940, and was producer and scriptwriter in the European Services from 1941 to 1955. Since 1963 he has been Head of Radio Drama. He was awarded the OBE in 1972. His previous publications include *Brecht: A Choice of Evils* (1951); *The Theatre of the Absurd* (1962); *Brief Chronicles. Essays on Modern Theatre* (1970); *Pinter. A Study of His Plays* (1973). He has also edited *Beckett* (1965), a collection of essays; *The Genius of the German Theatre* (1968); and *The New Theatre of Europe*

Modern Masters

BECKETT	A. Alvarez
CAMUS	Conor Cruise O'Brien
CHOMSKY	John Lyons
EINSTEIN	Jeremy Bernstein
ELIOT	Stephen Spender
FANON	David Caute
FREUD	Richard Wollheim
GANDHI	George Woodcock
GUEVARA	Andrew Sinclair
JOYCE	John Gross
JUNG	Anthony Storr
KAFKA	Erich Heller
KEYNES	D. E. Moggridge
LAING	Edgar Z. Friedenberg
LAWRENCE	Frank Kermode
LE CORBUSIER	Stephen Gardiner
LENIN	Robert Conquest
LÉVI-STRAUSS	Edmund Leach
LUKÁCS	George Lichtheim
MAILER	Richard Poirier
MARCUSE	Alasdair MacIntyre
MARX	David McLellan
MCLUHAN	Jonathan Miller
ORWELL	Raymond Williams
POPPER	Bryan Magee
POUND	Donald Davie
PROUST	Roger Shattuck
REICH	Charles Rycroft
RUSSELL	A. J. Ayer
SARTRE	Arthur C. Danto
SAUSSURE	Jonathan Culler
SCHOENBERG	Charles Rosen
WEBER	Donald MacRae
WITTGENSTEIN	David Pears
YEATS	Denis Donoghue

To be followed by

BARTHES	Annette Lavers
DOSTOYEVSKY	Harold Rosenberg
ENGELS	David McLellan
EVANS-PRITCHARD	Mary Douglas
GRAMSCI	James Joll
KLEIN	Hanna Segal
MERLEAU-PONTY	Hubert Dreyfus
NIETZSCHE	J. P. Stern
PAVLOV	J. A. Gray
SHERRINGTON	Jonathan Miller
TROTSKY	Irving Howe

Artaud

Martin Esslin

Fontana/Collins

First published in Fontana 1976
Copyright © Martin Esslin 1976
Made and printed in Great Britain by
William Collins Sons & Co Ltd Glasgow

Contents

Preface 7

1 Master or Madman? 9

2 The Road to Rodez 15

3 The Limits of Language 65

4 The Artaudian Theatre – Theory and
  Practice 76

5 More Devils than vast Hell can hold 96

6 Irrationalism, Aggression, Revolution 107

7 Conclusion 114

Notes 117

Chronology 119

Bibliography 125

Si je suis poète ou acteur ce n'est pas
pour écrire ou déclamer des poèsies,
mais pour les vivre.

Artaud, Letter to Henri Parisot,
6 October 1945

— Vous délirez, monsieur Artaud.
 Vous êtes fou.

— Je ne délire pas.
 Je ne suis pas fou . . .

Artaud, *Pour en finir avec le
judgement de Dieu*

Preface

Most books on Antonin Artaud hitherto available in English have concentrated on his theatrical theories and activity. The aim of this brief study of Artaud is somewhat different: while dealing with his views on the theatre at some length, it endeavours to set them within the wider framework of his importance as a cult figure, a revolutionary force and a unique psychological case history.

Artaud's work and his life are inextricably interwoven, hence a good deal of the book is devoted to an outline of his biography. A full chronology of his life is included as an appendix.

References to the collected edition of Artaud's work are given in the text; the title has been abbreviated as *OC* (i.e. *Oeuvres Complètes*), followed by the Roman numeral indicating the volume and Arabic figures giving the page. Quotations from *OC* in this book are from the first edition of volumes III-XIII, and from the 1970 revision of volume I and its supplementary volume, and from the 1973 edition of volume II. All translations from Artaud quoted in the text are my own, by permission of John Calder (Publishers) Ltd. Acknowledgements are due to Peter Owen Ltd and Harcourt Brace Jovanovich Inc. for permission to quote from *The Journals of Anaïs Nin*.

I am grateful to Dr R. D. Laing with whom I have discussed some of the implications of Artaud's psychiatric history. Needless to say, all views on this subject expressed in the book are nevertheless my own.

M.E.

1 Master or Madman?

A few months before he died Antonin Artaud was asked by the French radio service to prepare a programme for the series *La Voix des Poètes*; he wrote and recorded a radiophonic poem for four voices, xylophone and percussion which he called *Pour en finir avec le jugement de Dieu* (To Have Done with God's Judgement). It was due to be broadcast on 2 February 1948, but on 1 February the Director General of the Radiodiffusion Française banned it on the grounds that it was blasphemous and obscene and would prove intolerably offensive to the audience. Clearly the intention also was that the recording of this scandalous production should be destroyed. But surreptitious copies were made and have survived. One of these – eventually recopied on to a small cassette and therefore much deteriorated in quality – is in my possession. And so I can listen to Artaud's own voice as he recites his weird and violent words and utters his wild, piercing, inarticulate cries – outbursts of such a deep intensity of anguish beyond speech that they freeze the blood: it is as though all human suffering, mankind's sum-total of dammed-up, frustrated rage, torment and pain had been compressed into these tortured, primal shrieks.

It would be all too easy to dismiss these screams as no more than the demented ululations of a madman. That they contain an element of madness is beyond doubt; but there is also far more in them than mere madness. Yet – if it is not merely madness: what?

An answer to that question might furnish an explanation for the immense, surprising and by no means easily comprehensible impact Artaud has exercised on the generation which has grown up since he died in 1948, an impact which certainly qualifies him to be regarded as one of the 'modern masters', and which manifests itself in a number of different spheres: in the theatre, certainly, but also in poetry, literary criticism, psychology, political ideology, philosophy, the drug cult and the search for alternative life-styles. The very frequency with which Artaud's name is invoked in France, the

United States and many other Western countries makes him a figure whose influence must be recognised among the forces that shape the thinking and feeling of our time and, in some measure at least, contribute to its intellectual climate.

Yet if Artaud is among the modern masters, it is by no means easy to say into which of the recognised categories of achievement his contribution falls. He is not a *thinker* who could be regarded as having produced a coherent body of new knowledge or to have opened up new fields of inquiry; nor was he a *doer*, a man of action, a hero who has shaped events, influenced the course of history; and while, undoubtedly, he was a *poet* of great power, it is not his poetry that accounts for his influence. His writings about the *theatre* have had considerable influence, but his actual work in that sphere is generally acknowledged to have been a failure, so that he must be regarded as an inspiration for the work of others rather than a great director in his own right. In this he resembles those powerful figures who, while not producing anything like a tangible, verifiable system of thought, act as *catalysts* and *stimulators* for others by opening up new areas of speculation and directing the attention towards new modes of seeing – prophets of new visions like Nietzsche or Marshall McLuhan. Like these Artaud was the pioneer of a new approach, the inventor of a new vocabulary. This is a real and important contribution; but it still does not account for Artaud's wider, more profound influence in areas far removed from the theatre.

Artaud, I feel, is, above all, an example of another, more mysterious type of personality with major influence and impact: one of those masters whose impact arises not so much from what they have achieved and *done* in concrete, tangible terms, but rather from what they *are* and what they have *suffered*. The influence of powerful figures of this type ultimately derives from the image of themselves they have left behind and which has, somehow, mysteriously, become the encapsulated embodiment, clear, compressed, immediately apprehended, of a whole complex of attitudes, ideas and precepts contained within that image.

Such personalities radiate immense power and exercise far-reaching influence because their image has become a *symbol*, a concise poetic metaphor for their entire life, character and teaching. When one thinks of Artaud one is immediately aware of his image, or rather of one or the other of the two images which have come to stand for him and his life experience: the beautiful, spiritual young monk who stands by St Joan as she mounts the stake in Carl Theodor Dreyer's film *La Passion de Jeanne d'Arc*, the lean, ascetic face with its deep burning eyes captured in overwhelming close-ups; or the furrowed, ravaged face of the wasted, toothless old man that stares out of the self-portraits which Artaud himself drew in the last years of his life after he had emerged from a decade of confinement as a lunatic. Both these images remain engraved on the memory. They are unforgettable.

Artaud is unique among great writers and prophets in that he was an actor in the cinema so that his living, moving image remains as much with us as his recorded voice; and this has undoubtedly contributed to the emergence of his image as a power to be reckoned with and its crystallisation into the symbol of an attitude to life. For let it not be said that such a man's appearance is of no account. Artaud, the theoretician of the theatre who never tired of stressing the prime importance of the body's concrete reality as against the mere hot air of language and abstract thought, stands himself for the view that a man's looks may contain and express his essential truth. Would Che Guevara, an unsuccessful revolutionary and an unoriginal thinker, have ever acquired the influence he wielded among the young of the generation of 1968, had not his image, the beautiful, martyred face of his murdered body, captured the imagination and become the embodiment of a whole complex of doctrine, passion and life-style?

Some such symbol-images may acquire their power by mere chance. Artaud's does not belong to these. He shaped his image deliberately, fully conscious of what he was doing. Between the face of the soulful young monk of 1928 and the toothless, ravaged martyr's visage of 1948 there lies a lifetime of suffering which Artaud regarded as his ultimate artistic achievement: '*La tragédie sur la scène ne me suffit plus, je vais la transporter dans ma vie*' (Tragedy on the stage is not enough for me, I'll transfer it into my own life) he told Jean-Louis Barrault in 1935[1]. He designed his life, took upon himself and endured his suffering as a deliberate creation, a work of art. And the double image which remains with us, compresses and sums up his whole existence, *is*, in a certain sense, that work of art, or, at least, a metaphor for it.

Images of Man of such inner complexity, conciseness and expressive force are the stuff that myths are made of. Some such images are created by history itself and distil it into all-embracing, universally understood symbols: Saint Joan, the girl in soldier's garb riding at the head of liberating armies; Saint Sebastian pierced by arrows; Lenin orating, his head thrust forward, his arm raised in a fiery gesture. Other such myth-generating images are deliberate creations: Alfred Jarry turned into Ubu, an author becoming his own fiction; or Barbey d'Aurevilly, the eternal literary dandy, strolling through Paris with his lobster on the lead; or Chatterton who made himself the image of the martyred young poet. Such images-turned-into-myth can grow into objects of worship: what they all, each on its own level, have in common is, in fact, the mystery of *incarnation*: a body of ideas, precepts, experiences made concrete, become flesh; the story of a life and of a death compressed into one memorable picture capable of evoking an immediate emotional response. In such an image, the word, the concept is made palpable and becomes a physical presence. The incarnated Word, the Saviour on the Cross, is the greatest and most powerful of all these symbols. But the phenomenon exists on a multitude of levels, down to the humblest and most trivial. At the opposite end of the spectrum, the lowest rung of the ladder, stand the artificially created incarnations of the mass mind's aspirations, cult figures like James Dean or Marilyn Monroe.

Antonin Artaud, strangely, was both an actor *and* a prophet, an image on the flickering screen *and* a martyred saint, a figure in whom make-believe and profound aesthetic, philosophical, human insights mingle: a fine face, a sage, a teacher and a lunatic, all in one.

With his exceptional lucidity – the lucidity of the madman, some say – Artaud himself never doubted that his impact as an artist and as a teacher depended on his being able to incarnate his teaching and his art in his personality: '*Là où d'autres proposent des oeuvres, je ne prétends pas autre chose que de montrer mon esprit . . . je ne conçois d'oeuvre comme détachée de la vie (OCI, 49)* (Where others aspire to create works of art I do not want anything apart from showing my spirit . . . I cannot conceive of a work of art as distinct from life), he proclaimed as early as 1925, before he had reached the age of thirty.

Any attempt to present or understand Artaud must, therefore, take his life as its starting point. He is the true existential hero: what he did, what happened to him, what he suffered, what he *was* is infinitely more important than anything he said or wrote. Indeed so volatile, so contradictory are his opinions that it would be as easy to prove, by quotations from his published works or letters, that he was a deeply devout practising Christian as that he gloried in being a blaspheming atheist; that he preached violent revolution, as that he rejected all overt political action; that he saw salvation in sexual excess and the wildest indulgence of the senses, as that he regarded sexuality as the ultimate source of all the ills that beset mankind; that he was a leading Surrealist, as that he considered the whole movement as no better than a rabble of pretentious frauds; and, indeed, a whole row of further contradictory propositions. In fact, each such utterance can only be understood from the life situation, the existential context from which it sprang. It is futile to argue, as do those who regard Artaud as a useful prop of their particular cause, that he was lucid and in full command of his mental powers when he held the opinion they want to quote, and was utterly mad and unaware of what he was saying when he uttered the opposite view. The fact is that he held *all* his opinions with the same passionate sincerity at the moment he expressed them, and that it is impossible to draw a hard and fast line between his moments of 'sanity' and those of his 'madness', if, indeed, the concept of madness can be validly applied to a personality like Artaud at all.

But Artaud incarnates more, and more complex, concepts and problems than he himself could ever be aware of. His sufferings, for example, embody and exemplify, in an astonishingly clear and concentrated form, one of the most hotly debated and significant issues of our time: Artaud provides a focus and prime example for the controversy on the nature of insanity in which Michel Foucault in France and R. D. Laing and Thomas Szasz in the English-speaking world play so prominent a part, a controversy which raises issues far wider than mental health and contains a fundamental critique of our whole society and mode of life. Similarly Artaud, the drug addict and victim of drugs, incarnated, long before these

13

issues assumed their present importance, the whole complex and controversial problem of drugs and the drug culture.

There were times, during the years of his internment in various lunatic asylums, when Artaud was convinced that he was literally bearing the burden of the sins of all mankind; that he was starving because the people of the world were eating *his* food, that he was being poisoned by the sperm and excrement an entire impure world was unloading upon him. And when he finally succeeded in regaining his freedom, he identified himself with van Gogh, a great artist confined in lunatic asylums and driven to suicide by society. To our own time he has, even more so than van Gogh, become the embodiment of a lonely individual persecuted and victimised for his individuality and life-style by the upholders of convention and propriety. Hence his appeal to the radical, revolutionary Left. Persecuted, he replied with the rage of a ruthless persecutor. The immense, stored-up energies of boundless aggression which resound in the wild cries and screams on my tape are still fuelling the forces of radical dissent.

Such an ability to preserve and to release anew enormous psychic force is the hall-mark of the true myth. Artaud, the incarnation of a multitude of ideas and experiences is one of the archetypal, mythical heroes – or sacrificial victims – of our age. The creation of that myth and the image which embodies it is his life's achievement.

And – as with the heroes of all myths – the only way to gain access to an understanding of what he stands for, of what the image *means*, is to follow the story of the hero's life, martyrdom and death.

Antonin Marie Joseph Artaud was born at Marseilles – 4, Rue Jardin des Plantes – at eight o'clock on the morning of 4 September 1896.

Antoine Roi Artaud, his father, was a prosperous *armateur* or shipping agent whose business consisted in chartering ships for the trade with the Eastern Mediterranean, an area with which the family had close links. Artaud's paternal grandfather, Marius-Pierre Artaud had married a Greek from Asia Minor, Cathérine Schili (whose name was also spelt Schily, Schiley, Chili or Chilé). Artaud's mother, Euphrasie Nalpas, was the daughter of that Cathérine Schili's sister, Mariette Schili; his parents were thus first cousins, his two grandmothers sisters and he himself three-quarters Levantine Greek. Artaud remained deeply attached to his two grandmothers throughout his life. In his correspondence from the asylum at Rodez both make their appearance in the group of female figures – sometimes referred to as his daughters – whom he cherished with almost religious veneration.

In his childhood he occasionally accompanied his mother on her visits to Smyrna, where *her* mother, Mariette Nalpas née Schili (whom the family called Miette, and Artaud himself Neneka) lived. It was during one of these visits that, at the age of ten, he is said to have almost drowned in the sea, an incident which left him with a life-long fear and detestation of water. The Greek influence which pervaded Artaud's childhood can also be seen in the pet name by which he was known in the family, Nanaqui, derived from the Greek diminutive of his Christian name – Antonaki. He continued to use this name all his life and at times, when he strenuously denied that he was still Antonin Artaud, nevertheless remained Nanaqui to himself.

This link to the Levantine Greek world is more than a picturesque detail of Artaud's biography. It is a key factor in understanding his personality, outlook and mode of thinking. For while, undoubtedly, Artaud was formed in part by the literary and theatrical life of Paris – his friendships and feuds with the Surrealist circle and his contacts with the actors and directors around Dullin, Pitoeff and Jouvet – the Levantine world we know through Cavafy or Durrell's *Alexandria Quartet* also contributed its share to his development. The flamboyance of his acting style, even the way he pronounced certain vowels have, at times, been attributed to his origins. Nor can it be without significance that the one woman who played a major part in his emotional life, the actress Genica Athanasiou (1897-1966), a Rumanian of Albanian-Greek origin, came from the same Levantine background. When Artaud published his first poems in a little review he and some of his schoolfellows at the Collège du Sacré Coeur at Marseilles had started when he was about fourteen years old, he chose a pseudonym with a distinctly Greek flavour – Louis des Attides.

But the most striking expression of Artaud's immersion in the habits of thought and imagination of the Hellenistic world can be seen in the close affinity between his religious and cosmological fantasies in the last fifteen years of his life and the universe of the Hellenistic Gnostics, those numerous and diverse schools of philosophical and mystical speculation which flourished in the Eastern Mediterranean between the third and seventh centuries. Condemned and strenuously opposed by the Christian Churches as pernicious heretics, these Gnostic philosophers, schools and sects created a bewildering variety of syntheses between Christianity, Greek philosophy and Eastern religious thought and myth. Just as Artaud did in his later writings, the Gnostics mingled elements from the canonical as well as apocryphal books of the Bible with Neo-Platonism and the Cabbala, Indian beliefs in the transmigration of souls, the Egyptian cult of Osiris and Horus, Manichaean teachings about the world as a duality of good and evil, Zoroastrianism from Persia, Babylonian astrology which interprets the universe as a rigid hierarchy of ascending and descending spheres, and remnants of the classical Greek mystery religions like the cult of Dionysos and the mysteries of Orphism. In reading the writings of Artaud's final phase one is, again and again, struck by the parallels with Gnosticism: like Marcion of Halicarnassus Artaud believed that the God who created our world must be wicked and incompetent – how else could he have made it so cruel and imperfect? – and that salvation could only come from a God outside our universe and therefore innocent of its creation. Like the Barbelo-Gnostics who ritually spilled their sperm to break the endless cycle of sexual procreation, Artaud wanted to wean humanity away from the evil of physical sexuality; and like all the Gnostics he was obsessed with numerology, systems of divination and the making and breaking of spells. Artaud's strange book on the Roman Emperor Heliogabalus is dedicated to Apollonius of Tyana, the Greek philosopher who travelled through Asia Minor, Babylonia and India to merge Greek and Oriental doctrines. In his prophetic phase Artaud also saw himself as destined to reconcile Eastern philosophy and ritual with Western thought and art, and as an heir to the Hellenistic teachers and Magi who pursued the same ideal.

At the age of five Artaud fell severely ill. It is said that he had meningitis and that the disease left him with a nervous disability which remained with him all his life and was the source of most of his later sufferings. If this view is correct it would follow that Artaud's later psychological troubles had physiological causes. But such a connection should not, too easily, be taken for granted. Was the disease in question really meningitis? The diagnosis of meningitis was by no means too certain in 1901; the term as used then covered a multitude of fevers and infections. Moreover, Artaud himself, although he spoke of having suffered from headaches and facial cramps from between the ages of six and eight, dated the onset of his nervous debility from puberty. In 1914, when he was eighteen, he fell into an acute depression during which he destroyed all his youthful writings. This seems to indicate a profound emotional crisis rather than a purely physiological nervous disorder.

There may be a link between this adolescent emotional upheaval and an episode which Artaud endowed with great significance when looking back on his youth in the asylum at Rodez: at the age of nineteen (in 1915 or 1916), he maintained, he had been knifed in the back by two pimps in a street in Marseilles, Cours Devilliers. Whether this actually happened or not – Artaud tended to construct an imaginary and highly dramatic past for himself at this period – it did have reality for him as a turning point in his life. In 1945 – thirty years later – he regarded it as the first manifestation of a vast conspiracy by powerful sects of 'initiates' against him. The inner logic of this adventure, whether real or imaginary, seems to connect sexual guilt with the onset of the world's hostility towards him.

At Rodez Artaud claimed that the scar of that knife wound remained visible on his back. Whether he had been physically maimed or not, it was at about this time (1915/16) that he spent his first period in a sanatorium for nervous disorders at Rouguières near Marseilles.

The First World War was in its third year: after his return from the sanatorium Artaud, approaching the age of twenty, received his call-up papers. He spent nine months of 1916 in a military training camp at Digne; but eventually obtained his release from the army on medical grounds: he himself later used to say that it had been because of his sleep-walking.

Artaud's family tried, desperately, to obtain a cure for the nervous disability which prevented him from embarking on a career. During the next three years he spent long periods in a succession of resorts and sanatoria: at Saint-Dizier near Lyons, Lafoux-les-Bains (Gard), Divonne-les-Bains (Ain) and Bagnères-de-Bigorre in the Pyrenees. At the end of 1918 he was put into the care of Dr Dardel at a sanatorium at Le Chanet, near Neuchâtel, in Switzerland. Here he remained for well over a year, and here too he is said to have started to take laudanum. That date, May 1919, marks another fateful milestone in Artaud's life: the beginning of his enslavement to drugs.

Artaud's stay in Switzerland differed from his earlier sojourns in watering places and sanatoria in that Dr Dardel provided him with proper psychiatric care and treatment. As a result Artaud's state improved sufficiently to make it possible for him to go to Paris where his ambition was to embark on a literary career. Dr Dardel recommended that he should still remain under a degree of medical supervision and suggested that he might lodge with Dr Edouard Toulouse, at that time head psychiatrist of the asylum of Villejuif. Dr Toulouse was a pioneer of mental health and a man of high culture and a wide range of interests, literary and philosophical as well as scientific. As far back as 1912 he had created a literary periodical *Demain*, aimed at promoting a fuller, more integrated life-style on the basis of a fusion of scientific and 'moral' thought.

Dr Toulouse, as his wife reported later, recognised in Artaud, whose father brought him to Paris in March 1920, 'an exceptional being, of the race that produces a Baudelaire, a Nerval, a Nietzsche . . .' and, convinced that he was precariously balanced on a tightrope between genius and madness, decided to do his utmost to help him. Treating him as a member of the family, he gave him work which, while congenial, would not overtax him: revising the style of medical articles translated from the German, looking up facts in libraries; gradually he entrusted Artaud with the running of *Demain*. Here Artaud began to publish some of his poems, as well as contributing articles on a variety of subjects, such as a project for an improved form of the Baccalauréat, and theatre and art notices.

This literary activity and Dr Toulouse's connections in the artistic and intellectual circles of Paris opened doors for Artaud : he made the acquaintance of literary lions like the poet Max Jacob and met a number of prominent painters. And most important of all : ' Dr Toulouse introduced him to Lugné-Poe, the director of the Théâtre de l'Oeuvre. The dark young man with exquisite features greatly impressed Lugné-Poe (the producer who had launched Jarry's *Ubu Roi* on the world in 1896, the year Artaud was born) and Artaud became attracted to the idea of becoming an actor. By the end of 1920 he felt well enough to break loose from the direct supervision of Dr Toulouse and found himself lodgings in the 16th arrondissement. And Lugné-Poe offered him a small part in a forthcoming production.

On 17 February 1921 Artaud made his first appearance as an actor; in Henri de Régnier's *Les Scrupules de Sganarelle* he had a non-speaking role, a bourgeois woken from his slumbers by a disturbance in the night. Lugné-Poe praised him for the originality of his make-up and the elegance of his movement which made him appear as 'a painter who had strayed among actors'.

Artaud did not remain long at the Théâtre de l'Oeuvre. He continued his editorial activity with *Demain*, wrote poems and reviewed art exhibitions. In the summer he returned to Marseilles and spent a holiday with his family at Evian on the Lake of Geneva. Back in Paris in the autumn of 1921, however, he continued his efforts to become an actor. Artaud's uncle, Louis Nalpas, his mother's brother, was an influential figure in the French cinema of the time, artistic director of the Societé des Ciné-romans, well-known for producing novel-ettish films, the cinematic equivalents of the cheapest railway bookstall literature.

It was through Louis Nalpas that Artaud obtained an audition with the great actor Firmin Gémier (1869-1933) who had created the part of Ubu for Lugné-Poe in 1896 and was a tireless champion of the idea of a theatre for the people, which was realised after his death by Vilar's creation of the Théâtre National Populaire. Gémier had appeared in films produced by Louis Nalpas's company and was thus willing to give his nephew an audition. He was impressed by the young man and recommended him to Charles Dullin, who was just about to form his workshop of actors, half theatre school, half avant-garde ensemble, the Atelier. Dullin liked Artaud and offered him a place with the Atelier.

Charles Dullin – the outstanding French theatre personality of the nineteen twenties, a brilliant and highly intelligent director and an actor whose spirituality overcame the handi-cap of a far from impressive appearance – exercised a de-cisive influence on Artaud's thinking on the theatre. He was one of the first theoreticians of a *total theatre* in which ges-ture, mime, colour, music and movement would rival the dialogue in importance. Artaud had himself been thinking on similar lines. He waxed enthusiastic about a theatre 'in which there are no props. The Japanese are our immediate masters and inspiration, and in addition Edgar Poe . . .' (*OC III, 118*). He was deeply impressed by Dullin's intention 'that his performances should . . . give the impression of *things never seen before*. Everything takes place in the mind. The sets are even more stylised and deliberately shaped than at the Vieux Colombier. His idea is the Japanese actor who acts without props . . . The Gods of the school are not Tolstoy, Ibsen and Shakespeare but Hoffmann and Edgar Poe. Our first performance will display stern frenzy and demented sharp-ness . . . It is, to say the least, curious that I with my tastes should have stumbled on an enterprise so closely linked with my own ideas' (*OCIII, 121*).

In Dullin's troupe Artaud worked not only as an actor but also made use of his considerable talent as a draughtsman to design scenery and costumes.

Among the student-actors of the Atelier was Genica

Athanasiou, a young Rumanian actress who had come to Paris in 1919, at the age of twenty-two, to make her way in the theatre. Artaud fell wildly in love with her and their tempestuous affair lasted for some seven years through a series of crises usually provoked by Artaud's by no means unjustified jealousy. His love for Genica was so intense, so filled with a metaphysical fervour towards totality that she, a beautiful but mentally lazy and somewhat shallow woman, concerned about her career and wanting no more than a lover who could give her sexual fulfilment, could neither understand what he was after, nor live up to it.

The year 1922 was one of intense professional activity for Artaud the actor and designer. Dullin's troupe went on tour as well as appearing in Paris at the Vieux Columbier and elsewhere. After having played Anselme in Molière's *The Miser* in February, Artaud appeared in two important parts on 2 March : in Alexandre Arnoux's *Moriano et Galvan*, for which he had designed both the scenery and the costumes, he played the King of the Moors, Galvan, and, on the same evening, also appeared as Sottinet in Regnard's *Le Divorce*. For the third spectacle of the same evening, Lope de Rueda's interlude *Les Olives* he had designed the costumes. On 20 June he scored a critical success in another important part – Basilio, the King of Poland, in Calderón's *Life is a Dream*; Dullin played Prince Sigismund and Genica Athanasiou Estrella. Artaud had also designed the costumes. One newspaper remarked of Artaud that he had managed to combine great simplicity with marvellous royal dignity.

For the summer Artaud returned to Marseilles where, at the Colonial Exhibition, he was deeply impressed by a troupe of Cambodian dancers who performed in a reconstruction of the Temple of Angkor, an experience which foreshadows the even more decisive experience of his discovery of Balinese Dance Theatre at the Paris Colonial Exhibition of 1931.

In October Dullin finally moved into a permanent home for his theatre, the building on the Place Dancourt on Montmartre which became famous as the Théâtre de l'Atelier. And again Artaud continued to play important roles. But he began to annoy Dullin by insisting on more and more bizarre interpretations of his parts. In Pirandello's *Pleasure of Honesty*, in which he was playing a member of the board of directors of a commercial enterprise, he appeared made up in the highly stylised manner of the classical Chinese theatre. 'A symbolical make-up slightly out of place in a modern comedy'[1] was Dullin's view more than a quarter-century later. In Alexandre Arnoux's *Huon de Bordeaux* Artaud played the Emperor Charlemagne. During a rehearsal he entered on all fours and crawled towards his throne like an animal. Dullin disagreed with this extravagant interpretation of the old emperor's character and tried to stop him. Artaud suddenly got up and said with a gesture of utter contempt: 'Oh well! If you insist on truth!' (*Oh! Si vous travaillez dans la verité! Alors!*)

Nevertheless he achieved considerable success and earned Dullin's approval in some other productions, notably Cocteau's *Antigone* which opened on 20 December 1922 and attracted 'tout Paris'. Genica Athanasiou appeared in the title role, Artaud was Tiresias and Dullin Creon. Picasso designed the set, Coco Chanel the costumes, the music was by Arthur Honegger. The first night, moreover, produced a typically Parisian scandal. Two different bands of opponents of Cocteau tried to stop the performance: Raymond Duncan, Isadora's brother, who felt that Cocteau had betrayed the true Greek spirit, and André Breton and his Surrealists who deplored Cocteau's descent into the world of fashion.

After his clash with Dullin over his interpretation of Charlemagne Artaud left the Atelier and joined Georges Pitoeff's troupe at the Comédie des Champs-Elysées. Jean Hort, a Swiss actor also with Pitoeff at the time, describes him as looking barely older than twenty, although he was already approaching twenty-seven. But on stage, while acting, Hort says, his intensity, the feverish tension which stiffened his body, enabled him to appear much older, indeed any age he wanted. 'I can still see', says Hort, 'the pale colour of his face, his shadowed cheeks in which repeated tensing had not yet cut permanent lines. His chestnut hair still grew deep into his forehead, which later, once it was bare, would look so remarkable. I can still see his blue-green eyes, often feverish, his frail body . . . And his hands!'[2]

At the Comédie des Champs-Elysées Artaud appeared in a number of supporting parts (he was cast as the prompter in Pirandello's *Six Characters in Search of an Author* but failed to turn up at the final rehearsals and had to be replaced;

later he was allowed to take up his part again; as Jackson in Leonid Andreyev's *He Who Gets Slapped*; and as a Robot in Capek's *RUR*, directed by Kommissarjevsky). In 1924 he also acted in two films (Claude Autant-Lara's *Faits Divers* and Luitz-Morat's *Surcouf*, shot on location in Brittany in the summer; in this he had the important part of a villainous traitor). An acting task which combined theatre and film was the first performance of Ivan's Goll's *Methusalem* at the Théâtre Michel, an avantgarde play which included filmed passages (in these, directed by Jean Painlevé, Artaud appeared as an officer, a bishop and a country bumpkin).

While establishing himself as a man of the theatre and making his mark in the cinema, Artaud continued his literary activity. His poems appeared in such periodicals as the *Mercure de France* and *Action* as well as Dr Toulouse's *Demain*: he edited an anthology of the writing of Dr Toulouse, *Au fil des préjugés*, which was published in 1923. And D. H. Kahnweiler, the famous art dealer and publisher, whom he had met through his artist friends André Masson, Elie Lascaux, and Joan Miró, issued Artaud's first book, a slim volume of poems *Tric-Trac du Ciel* (the title has been rendered as 'Backgammon of the Heavens' which sounds much less poetic than the French) in an edition limited to one hundred copies.

But the most important development, decisive for Artaud's entire career, was his famous correspondence with Jacques Rivière, the influential editor of the *Nouvelle Revue Française*, France's leading literary periodical. Artaud had sent some of his poems to the *NRF* and on 1 May 1923 Rivière replied that he felt unable to publish them. Yet they had aroused his interest sufficiently to want to make their author's acquaintance: could Artaud pass by at his convenience any Friday between four and six? On 5 June Artaud went to see Rivière. The same evening he wrote him a long letter to reply to the criticisms of his work which Rivière had made during their conversation. Artaud admitted the weakness of his poems but went on to explain his peculiar difficulty:

I am suffering from a terrible sickness of the spirit. My thought abandons me in all possible measure, from the simple fact of the thought itself to the external fact of its materialisation in words. Words, the shape of sentences,

23

the internal direction of thoughts, simple reactions of the mind – I am in constant pursuit of my intellectual being. When, therefore *I can take hold of a shape*, however imperfect, I set it down, out of fear that I might lose the whole idea. I am below my own level, I know it, I suffer from it, but I submit to it rather than die altogether. (*OCI*, 30).

Artaud, it must be stressed, did not adduce this argument, that he suffered from a nervous disorder, in mitigation of a lack of talent. He drew Rivière's attention to the fact that what he wanted to say did not amount to a mere personal apologia, but raised important general questions: was writing which emerged from a tremendous struggle for expression and was therefore less than perfect in form and elegance really less deserving of publication than more facile but formally more perfect poems? Rivière's reply showed that he had not grasped this point at all. It merely reassured Artaud that with a little application he might well do better and get published in the *NRF*. More than six months later on 29 January 1924 Artaud, who had obviously been pondering Rivière's insensitive consolatory remarks, returned to the attack: were not the products of such a profound struggle for expression of real worth? 'I am a man who has suffered much in his mind, and because of this *I have the right* to speak' (*OCI*, 38). And he included a new poem *Cri*. No reply was received and on 24 March 1924 Artaud curtly demanded the return of his letters and manuscripts. On the following day Rivière replied, apologetically. He recognised the interest of Artaud's work. But, he asked, how was it possible, if Artaud really had such difficulties in catching the flow of his thought in the act of setting it down on paper, that, in describing this very disability, he could reach such heights of lucidity and eloquence? Rivière warned Artaud against literary theories which insisted on extreme spontaneity of expression, such as that of the Surrealists, and advised him, in a rather patronising manner, to work hard at trying to perfect his ability to translate his thoughts into formal patterns. The correspondence continued till 8 June and the upshot of it all was that Rivière suggested that instead of publishing the poems Artaud had sent him, he should publish the correspondence about the *rejection* of the poems.

Rivière wanted Artaud to remain anonymous, but Artaud insisted that nothing should be concealed.

The *Correspondence avec Jacques Rivière* appeared in the *NRF*'s number for September 1924 and, later, as a book. It is of prime importance not merely because it made Artaud's name well known and enabled him to become a contributor to the most influential organ of the French intellectual elite, but above all because it marks the decisive breakthrough for his development as a writer. At last he had found a subject to write about: his own case, his disability as a paradigm of the problem of art itself. Rivière's rejection had provoked him into an examination of his own problem and the realisation that this predicament was of general import and significance. Only a few months earlier, in a note in a small occasional periodical he had started in February 1923 (*Le Bilboquet* – only two numbers ever appeared), Artaud had felt quite differently about the problem of capturing thought in poetry and had, in effect, shared Rivière's view that it was all a matter of hard work and technique:

> The supreme art consists in lending to the expression of our thought the rigour and truth of its original stratification through the cunning of a well-applied rhetoric. . . . And the art consists in bringing this rhetoric to the point of crystallisation needed to achieve a complete fusion with certain modes of being, real ones, of the emotion and the thought. – In a word: the only enduring writer is the one who has been able to make that rhetoric behave as though it *was* the thought itself, and not just the outward form (*geste*) of the thought. (*OCI*, 269)

In the correspondence with Rivière, on the other hand, Artaud not only acknowledged the fact that he found it impossible to capture his emotion and his thought in the act of writing, (which would have been no more than a personal, and highly regrettable, disability) but insisted that writing which recorded that failure, or, indeed, the impossibility of ever achieving complete success in capturing the thought itself, transcended the shallow and facile achievements of those who used rhetoric to mask that impossibility. (There are close parallels here to Beckett's attitude to writing as a pursuit not of success but of a minimalisation of failure.)

The correspondence with Rivière revealed Artaud to himself: for the first time he had found a theme of his own rather than following the conventional lines of writing poetry about organ grinders' monkeys, the freshly-fallen snow or, indeed, Love. The new theme he had found was himself, his own case. In the following year he published two slim volumes of miscellaneous writings, which clearly show this shift towards his new subject matter. These are *L'Ombilic des Limbes* (a title difficult to translate, perhaps best rendered as 'The Navel [i.e. focal point or centre] of Limbo') which appeared in July 1925; and *Le Pèse-Nerfs* (no easier to translate, perhaps: 'Scales on which to weigh one's nerves'), which followed in August. The opening sentence of *L'Ombilic des Limbes* shows how far Artaud had moved from the conventional concept of the poet and man of letters: 'Where others want to produce works of art, I aspire to no more than to display my own spirit' (*OCI, 61*). And *Le Pèse-Nerfs* contains repeated assertions of Artaud's newly-won awareness and pride of being a special case: 'I am he who has most closely experienced the numbing dislocation of his language in relation to his thought' (*OCI, 119*); and his contempt for those whose main objective is fine writing: 'All writing is swinishness. People who venture forth to try to put down in precise terms anything that goes on in their thought, are swine . . .' (*OCI, 120*).

Artaud's formal adherence to the Surrealist movement, a few weeks after the publication of his correspondence with Rivière, can also be seen as the direct and logical consequence of this rejection of the conventional notion of 'literature'. Once the laborious process of fixing thought and emotion through the application of technique and skill, *art* is unmasked as mere pretence and sham; once the movement of the mind in forming the emotion and the thought is recognised as more important than the elegance and refinement of its expression; then *automatic writing* as preached, if not always practised by the Surrealists, would be the answer. Artaud was introduced to the Surrealists by André Masson. From October 1924 he began to take an active part in the Surrealist movement: he contributed to periodicals like *La Révolution Surréaliste* and *Disque Vert* and in January 1925 became director of the Surrealist Bureau de Recherches. Apart from passionate discussions about the content of the Surrealist philosophy, the work of this research department consisted in collecting material (automatic writing, dreams), in trying to evolve 'means and ways for a Surrealist investigation within the confines of Surrealist thought' (*OCI*, 344) and to establish criteria by which authentically Surrealist thought could be recognised.

Artaud was nominated editor for the third issue of *La Révolution Surréaliste* (15 April 1925) and himself wrote a considerable number of the texts it contained. The cover announced boldly that 1925 was 'The End of the Christian Era'. Inside there were letters written by Artaud to the Pope and the Chancellors of Europe's universities which rejected both Christianity and Western logic; they were followed by letters to the Dalai Lama and to the Buddhist schools, begging them to assist in the elimination of Western ways : 'Teach us, o Lama, the material levitation of the body and how we can no longer be held down by the earth' (*OCI*, 340), 'Like you [the schools of Buddha] we reject progress : come, and overthrow our habitations' (*OCI*, 343).

While engaged in intense activity on behalf of the Surrealists and in close personal contact with André Breton, Robert Desnos, Aragon, Eluard, Max Ernst, Raymond Queneau and many other stimulating personalities, Artaud had to pursue his acting career in films. His father had died on 7 September 1924, a few weeks before he joined the Surrealist group. This meant the cessation of financial help from Marseilles. Artaud's mother moved to Paris where she lived in relatively modest circumstances, and Artaud had to earn his own living. The cinema seemed the likeliest source of a steady income, particularly as Artaud's uncle, who had helped him to gain a foothold in the industry was pleased with his nephew's successes. In June 1925 Artaud spent some weeks in Italy on location for a film by Marcel Vandal (*Graziella*), in August he worked on Luitz-Morat's *Le Juif Errant*. But the theatre remained Artaud's main concern. Among the Surrealists he encountered was the playwright Roger Vitrac who shared many of Artaud's ideas and ambitions. In the course of 1926 they gradually formulated an idea for an avantgarde theatre devoted to the exploration of dramatic ideas linked with the Surrealist concept, a theatre of the fantastic and grotesque, of dream and obsession, to be called Théâtre Alfred Jarry.

Vitrac, Artaud and Robert Aron approached Dr René

Allendy and his wife Yvonne on 26 September 1926 with a request to help them in raising money for this venture. René Allendy is another of the enlightened psychiatrists (like Dr Toulouse and later Dr Ferdière at Rodez) who played such an important part in Artaud's life. A well-known psycho-analyst (Artaud briefly underwent some sessions of treatment with him in 1927), he was also interested in para-psychology and occultism and was head of a *Groupe d'Etudes Philosophiques et Scientifiques pour l'Examen des Tendances Nouvelles* at the Sorbonne. His wife, Yvonne, a woman of great charm and intelligence, was greatly interested in the arts. She decided to assist Artaud, Vitrac and Aron (who acted as the administrator of the project) and succeeded in raising 3000 francs.

In its issue for November 1926 the *Nouvelle Revue Française* (edited, after the death of Jacques Rivière in February 1925, by Jean Paulhan, who became a close friend of Artaud's and played an important part in his life) published the *First Manifesto of the Théâtre Alfred Jarry*. This already contains a good many of Artaud's later ideas about a theatre of cruelty. If theatre was merely play the world was too serious a place to indulge in it. 'If the theatre is not just play, if it is a genuine reality, by what means can we give it that status of reality, make each performance a kind of event? That is the problem we have to solve' (*OCI, 11*). As an example of the kind of spectacle which is both theatrical and real the manifesto cites a police raid on a brothel, with the ballet-like deployment of the force surrounding the premises, followed by the procession of the arrested whores being led away like cattle to the slaughter. 'This is what we want to arrive at: that at each performance we take a grave risk, that the whole interest of our effort lies in its seriousness. It is not to the mind or the senses of our audience that we address our-selves, but to their whole existence. Theirs and ours' (*OCII, 13*). So that ultimately the audience 'will go to the theatre as [they] go to the surgeon or the dentist' (*OCII, 15*). The leaflet issued by the new group to announce its first season (1926/7) promised, among other things, several hitherto un-performed plays by Jarry, *The Revenger's Tragedy* by Tour-neur and Strindberg's *Dream Play*. Not all of these projects came to fruition.

The preparations for the Théâtre Alfred Jarry brought

Artaud into conflict with the Surrealists. As early as September 1925, less than a year after he had joined them, Artaud wrote to Genica Athanasiou that he had received a hectoring letter from Breton 'about Vitrac, in which he treats him as a villain and more or less orders me to break with him'.[3] Vitrac had quarrelled with Eluard and had been expelled by the Surrealists in December 1924. As Artaud's association with Vitrac became closer, the Surrealists began to taunt him for his supposed commercialism in continuing to appear as a film actor and in trying to launch a theatrical enterprise of his own. And when Breton and his followers decided to convert the purely literary Surrealist revolution into a political one and announced their collective adherence to the Communist Party, the break became inevitable.

At the end of November 1926, at a meeting held in the café 'Le Prophète', Artaud and Philippe Soupault were formally expelled by the Surrealists. The language used about Artaud in the official document listing his transgression is extremely strong. Calling him a man animated by a veritable beastliness, they accused him 'that he wanted to see in the Revolution no more than a change of the internal conditions of the soul, an attitude which belongs to the feeble-minded the impotent and the cowardly. Never, in whatever field, did his activity (he was also a film actor) constitute anything but concessions to nullify . . . Let us leave him to his disgusting mixture of dreams, vague assertions, pointless insolence and manias . . .' (*OCI, 445*). As a final insult the document hinted that Artaud was not beyond committing the ultimate transgression, re-conversion to the Christian faith. Although this actually happened some ten years later, the only grounds for assuming such a step in 1926 were some contacts Artaud had had with Jacques Maritain.

This document was not made public at the time. But Breton, Aragon, Eluard, Péret and Unik jointly signed a pamphlet (probably written by Breton) *Au grand jour* (In Broad Daylight) in which they announced their adherence to the Communist Party and the expulsion of Artaud and Soupault. Artaud replied, in the summer of 1927, in a pamphlet of his own, *A la grande nuit ou Le Bluff surréaliste* in which he hit back with equal ferocity: '. . . Did not Surrealism die the day when Breton and his adepts thought they had to join Communism and to seek, in the realm of fact and matter, the fulfilment of an endeavour which could not normally develop anywhere but in the inner recesses of the brain' (*OCI*, 364). Artaud insisted that the social, material, *external* plane was of no interest to him because it was only a pale reflection of inner realities.

In spite of the bitterness of these exchanges, Artaud's name still occasionally made an appearance in Surrealist publications. And to the end of his life André Breton was one of the people he remained most attached to, and who played an important part in his fantasy life at Rodez.

Film acting, so despised by the Surrealists, continued to occupy and maintain Artaud in funds. 1927 brought him two of his most famous roles: Marat in Abel Gance's *Napoléon* and the part of the friar who accompanies St Joan to the stake in Carl Theodor Dreyer's great film *La Passion de Jeanne d'Arc*. He also appeared as a young intellectual soldier in Léon Poirier's *Verdun, visions d'histoire* and was much attacked for this by the left intelligentsia of Paris, as the film had been launched with official support as a patriotic work. And he became interested in the cinema as an art form which might be used to realise some of the ideas of the Surrealists. In November 1927 the *Nouvelle Revue Française* published his script for such a film, *La Coquille et le Clergyman* (The Seashell and the Clergyman), which actually went into production under the direction of Germaine Dulac, one of the earliest women directors in the history of the cinema. But Artaud was deeply dissatisfied with Dulac's approach to his script, which, although bizarrely unrealistic, he wanted to have treated as real, but which she had transformed into a series of dream images. When the film was shown for the first time at the Studio des Ursulines on 18 February 1928, Artaud and some of his friends tried to stop the performance by shouting insults about the director. Later, when Bunuel's *L'Age d'Or* and *Le Chien Andalou*, and Cocteau's *Le Sang d'un Poète* were hailed as pioneer works of a cinema of dream images, Artaud angrily drew attention to the fact that his film had preceded all these and was, in fact, much better than any of them.

In the meantime the Théâtre Alfred Jarry had come into being. It had neither a permanent company, nor a permanent home, and consisted of no more than its three initiators who planned, from case to case, to present their productions with ad hoc companies in theatres hired for a few evenings. The first presentation was a triple bill: a short play *Gigogne* by Max Robur (pseudonym for Robert Aron); a musical joke by Artaud *Le Ventre Brûlé ou la Mère Folle*, the text of which has been lost (it is said to have been a humorous treatment of the conflict between the cinema and the theatre, one critic describing it as 'a short hallucination with hardly any text in which the author has condensed a synthesis of life and death' and adding that 'it left an extremely strong and persistent impression of strangeness' (*OCIV*, 380); and a major Surrealist, or rather proto-Absurdist, play by Vitrac, *Les Mystères de l'Amour*. Rehearsals started in May 1927 in the Théâtre de l'Atelier which Dullin had put at the group's disposal; the performances were to be at the Théâtre de Grenelle, in which only one final rehearsal could be held during the night before the opening.

Two performances took place of this first production of the Théâtre Alfred Jarry (1 and 2 June 1927). The press was by no means unfavourable, but it would be an exaggeration to say that the venture had an impact much greater than similar experimental showcase productions usually had in Paris. Aron was left with a deficit of almost 7000 francs, which he covered out of his own pocket.

But, while Artaud tried to earn his living in films, the activities of the Théâtre Alfred Jarry continued. On 14 January 1928 it mounted its second presentation at the Comédie des Champs-Elysées. This was an even more curious mixture. One half of the programme consisted of the uncut version of Pudovkin's film version of Gorki's *The Mother*, one of the masterpieces of the Soviet cinema, the showing of which in cinemas had been banned by the censor. The other half of the evening was a stage presentation of what was announced as 'one act of a play, the name of whose author we are withholding, and who, incidentally has not authorised us to perform it'. Taken out of context the long dialogues of this fragment of a play appeared incomprehensible and boring to the audience, who became restless and loudly voiced their dissatisfaction. The play was in fact the third act of Claudel's *Partage de Midi*, and the intention, clearly, was to expose its wordiness and boredom and to hold it up to ridicule. Breton, who was in the audience, was among the first to realise this, and shouted: 'Shut up, you idiots, this is by

Claudel!'. After the curtain had come down, Artaud appeared in front of it and announced: 'The play is by Paul Claudel, Ambassador of France – who is an infamous traitor!'. The Surrealists who were present in force were in raptures and it looked as though they would forgive Artaud many past sins and insults. But the rest of the audience and the establishment press were deeply scandalised and indignant. So also was the *Nouvelle Revue Française*, Claudel's publisher whose copyright had been breached and to whom Artaud owed so much for publicising his theatrical venture. Even Artaud's relationship with Génica Athanasiou suffered. He had made her act the part of Ysé without letting her know who had written the play and quarrelled with her over the interpretation of the text. On the other hand, the scandal had achieved one objective: it had made Artaud and his enterprise well known.

If scandal was the objective, the next venture of the group again attained it. But this time it was not the establishment but the Surrealists who were scandalised. Artaud had from the very beginning planned to produce Strindberg's *Dream Play*. Mme Allendy had friends among the Swedish colony in Paris and it was suggested that the Swedish Embassy might subsidise the production of a play by a great Swedish writer. Artaud agreed. He secured an excellent cast which included Tania Balachova, Raymond Rouleau, and Etienne Decroux (later to become famous as a great mime). Two performances were planned, to be held on 2 and 9 June 1928 at the Théâtre de l'Avenue. The first of these was a brilliant society occasion: the Swedish Ambassador, Prince George of Greece, the Duchess of Rochefoucauld, Paul Valéry and hosts of foreign journalists were present. But so were some thirty Surrealists who occupied the front rows of the stalls. Furious that Artaud had accepted subsidies from a foreign government and allied himself with the cream of society, these Surrealist interlopers hurled insults at the actors about being in the pay of Swedish capitalism. Artaud replied from the stage that he had only agreed to produce it because Strindberg himself had been a victim of the Swedish establishment. At this some Swedes walked out of the theatre. It was a memorable scene.

But worse was to come – from the Surrealists' point of view the ultimate in abject treason on Artaud's part. The second performance was to be held a week after the first one, as a matinée on 9 June. Artaud and Aron, afraid that the disturbances would recur, announced that they were resolved to employ all means at their disposal to stop such a repetition. And these means consisted of – the police. Breton, Sadoul, Unik and other Surrealists were arrested at the entrance. And, according to Breton, Artaud himself was at the door, pointing his erstwhile friends out to '*les flics*'.

Robert Aron had had enough. He withdrew. But Vitrac and Artaud soldiered on to mount one more production. This was Vitrac's own play *Victor ou Les Enfants au pouvoir*, without doubt the only truly important new play presented by the Théâtre Alfred Jarry. This brilliant piece which presents the plot of a conventional French bedroom farce as seen through the eyes of a hyper-intelligent child, unable to fathom the mysteries of sex which prompt his elders to behave in such an irrational fashion, gave Artaud an excellent opportunity to shine as a director. Tania Balachova was again in the cast. The actress, who was to play Ida Mortemart, the beauty afflicted with an irrepressible urge to fart, withdrew in horror. In a letter printed in the programme Artaud explained to her replacement, Domenica Blazy, that this character represents the intrusion of the sordid side of matter into the realm of spiritual beauty. *Victor* was given three performances at the Comédie des Champs-Elysées, on 24 and 29 December 1928 and 5 January 1929. Many of the critics were shocked, very few saw the power and originality of the play and production. One of them gave it curious conditional praise : if it were true that *Ubu Roi* is a masterpiece, then *Victor*, which could be regarded as a kind of sequel to *Ubu*, might also be seen as a masterpiece! Foreign correspondents in Paris, less committed to the conventions of the French theatre, saw the matter more clearly. Paul Block, of the *Berliner Tageblatt* called it the most curious theatrical experience he had had in eight years as a correspondent in France; and the correspondent of *Lidove Noviny* of Prague clearly saw that the *leitmotiv* of *Victor* was the human condition itself, subject as it is to being soiled by the impurity of matter.

Victor, the fourth production of the Théâtre Alfred Jarry, was also its last. The Vicomte de Noailles gave Artaud another 20,000 francs in November 1929 to enable him to carry on, but even this sum proved insufficient. For the next six years Artaud desperately tried to regain an opportunity to direct a play on the Paris stage. And when he finally succeeded, in 1935, it led to catastrophe for him.

Having suffered a reversal in the theatre, Artaud fell back on the cinema. He desperately needed money, not least to enable him to relaunch his theatrical ventures. He had hopes of selling some film scripts and, through these, breaking into film production. With this aim in mind he wrote a film treatment of R. L. Stevenson's *The Master of Ballantrae* (which he registered with the Association des Auteurs du Film on 26 April 1929) and made a free translation of Lewis's Gothick novel *The Monk*, published as a book in 1931. None of these film projects ever materialised. But Artaud's acting career continued. He appeared in an adaptation of Zola's *L'Argent*, directed by Marcel Herbier, and spent several months in the spring of 1929 in Nice, playing the part of a gipsy in Raymond Bernard's highly successful epic *Tarakanova*. In the early years of talking pictures some European companies produced their films in two versions in different languages, using the same sets and costumes. This practice was particularly popular in Germany and Artaud went to Berlin several times to take part in the French versions of German productions. One of these, in 1930, was G. W. Pabst's film of Brecht's *Threepenny Opera*. The version of this classic which is usually shown is the German one with Rudolf Forster as Mac the Knife and Carola Neher as Polly. But a French version of the *Opéra de Quat' Sous* also exists with Albert Préjean as Mac the Knife. In this version Artaud plays the young man at the very beginning of the film who asks Peachum to join his organisation of beggars and is shown the methods by which human pity can be aroused. Artaud's life thus touches that of Brecht. Like Brecht, Artaud disliked Pabst's adaptation of the play; but he admired Brecht's work.

Artaud found Berlin fascinating. 'If I did not suffer from my perpetual headaches' he wrote to Dr Allendy in July 1930, 'I should greatly enjoy the life of Berlin, a city of astonishing luxury and frightening licentiousness. I am constantly amazed by what I see. They carry their obsession with eroticism everywhere, even into the shop-windows in which all the dummies thrust their bellies forward . . .' (*OCIII*, *193*). Artaud made several more visits to Berlin between 1931 and 1935. During the war, at Rodez, he claimed that he had met

Hitler in the Romanisches Café, the meeting place of actors and intellectuals. This may well have been no more than one of the fantasies in which he indulged in that period in the asylum. But it may well also have been true. There is no reason why Hitler should not have occasionally been seen in the *Romanisches Café*.

The films in which Artaud was cast became worse and worse (he mainly worked for Raymond Bernard, Tristan Bernard's son – *Faubourg Montmartre, Les Croix de Bois* – and Marcel Herbier – *La Femme de Nuit*); nor did he get enough work in the cinema to give him an acceptable income. So his struggle to make a living became more and more desperate. As far back as March 1928 he had been invited by Dr Allendy's study group to lecture at the Sorbonne on *Art and Death*; a year later Robert Denoel published a little book with the same title, *L'Art et la Mort*, which contains a number of texts which had previously appeared in periodicals. Only the opening meditation had not previously been published but it seems too short to have formed a complete lecture and may merely be a fragment of that lecture. It is chiefly remarkable for extolling the utility of drugs to recreate that state of mind of extreme lucidity of which children alone are spontaneously capable.

Artaud also contributed short notes and reviews to the *Nouvelle Revue Française* and even wrote, to make some money, fake first-hand reports of the Galapagos Islands and the brothels of Shanghai for the magazine *Voilà*.

Yet he never lost sight of his main objective: to revolutionise the theatre. In July 1931 he visited the Colonial Exhibition in the Bois de Vincennes and had one of the key experiences of his life: on the terrace of the Indonesian temple which housed the exhibit of the Dutch colonial empire he saw a performance of Balinese dancing. Artaud was deeply moved: here all his ideas of a non-verbal, magical theatre of light, colour and movement seemed realised. His article on the Balinese theatre, later reprinted in *The Theatre and its Double*, appeared in the *Nouvelle Revue Française* for October 1931. This initiated a series of theoretical essays on the theatre, some originally delivered as lectures at the Sorbonne, which later formed the basis of Artaud's most influential book, *The Theatre and its Double*.

From 1931 Artaud embarked on a desperate search for

the means to start his own theatre. At the beginning of 1932 he succeeded in persuading Louis Jouvet to allow him to assist in the production of a play by Alfred Savoir, *La Patissière du Village*. But Artaud spoiled his chances of gaining a foothold in an established theatre by putting forward extravagant ideas, which that conventional play simply could not support. In a letter to Jouvet (5 February 1932) he suggested that in the dream scene at the end of the play some twenty giant puppets, each more than fifteen feet in height, should appear, swaying to the tune of a military march, made strange by the admixture of oriental harmonies, while Bengal fireworks exploded all around them. These puppets should each carry a symbolical object: one of them, for example, could have the Arc de Triomphe on its shoulders. No wonder that Jouvet got frightened and dropped Artaud.

Undaunted Artaud approached Dullin and suggested that he should be allowed to direct Buechner's *Woyzeck*, one of his favourite plays. In a letter to Jean Paulhan, the editor of the *NRF* who had collaborated on the translation of *Woyzeck*, dated 7 March 1932, Artaud mentions this plan and adds that he had found a patron who might give money towards a project 'which might be for the theatre what the *NRF* is for literature'. Artaud felt that this patron, Monsieur de Grinief, director of the Comptoir National Cinématographique, could be persuaded to finance the venture if it found the support of the leading intellectuals around the *NRF*, André Gide, Paul Valéry, Valéry Larbaud, Julien Benda and, of course, Paulhan himself, as well as Gaston Gallimard, the head of the *NRF* publishing enterprise. Paulhan was not unsympathetic. He agreed to publish an article by Artaud which would be a programme and manifesto for such a new theatre.

But the whole project was prematurely leaked to the press. On 26 June 1932 the *Intransigeant* published an article by Henri Philippon headed *Le Théâtre de la NRF* in which he reported rumours that the *NRF* had decided to open a theatre and that they had, after much heart-searching chosen Artaud to direct it:

It was at the Café des Deux-Magots that I had the good fortune of running into M. Antonin Artaud.

– 'I hear whispers that the Nouvelle Revue Française wants to start a theatre. Is that true?'

– 'Evidently, I myself am to run it. In a forthcoming number of the NRF I shall be publishing a kind of manifesto which André Gide, Julien Benda, Albert Thibaudet, Jean Paulhan and Jules Supervielle will countersign. They will form the committee of honour.' (*OCV*, 298)

On the following day the *Intransigeant* published a letter from Artaud headed 'The Theatre I am about to start' in which he explained some of his ideas more fully and also tactfully suggested that it was not the *NRF* who had initiated the project, but that *he* was doing so with the assistance of some of the writers connected with the journal. But the harm had been done. Gallimard was furious and Artaud had to apologise to him. Nevertheless the *NRF* did publish the *First Manifesto of the Theatre of Cruelty* in its number dated October 1932.

There had been much debate between Paulhan and Artaud about the name by which Artaud's venture should be known. Artaud had written an article for publication in the journal *SUR* of Buenos Aires with the title *Le Théâtre Alchimique* (the Alchemical Theatre). Paulhan thought that might be a better name; he also suggested Theatre of the Absolute or Metaphysical Theatre. But Artaud insisted on Theatre of Cruelty.

The response to this manifesto for a new theatre was, to say the least, lukewarm. Bernard Steele, the publisher, tried to launch a *Societé Anonyme du Théâtre de la Cruauté* with a total capital of 100,000 francs in 100-franc shares. Later, after the publication of Artaud's *Second Manifesto of the Theatre of Cruelty*, the projected share capital was raised to 650,000 francs. But this was even less successful.

To provide material for his theatrical enterprise, should it ever come to fruition, Artaud worked on a number of outlines of productions that would fit in with his ideas. In 1932 he was busy on an adaptation of Seneca's tragedy of *Atreus and Thyestes*; in 1933 he produced a scenario for a *Conquest of Mexico*, which, to raise funds, he read at a soirée which Lise Deharme gave for him in her home on the Quai Voltaire, on 6 January 1934. He was also thinking of a play based on Shelley's *The Cenci*.

Artaud's liaison with Genica Athanasiou had come to an end after the quarrel over *Partage de Midi* at the beginning of 1928. He continued to see her sporadically. In 1930/31 he lived for a time with Josette Lusson, an actress who had also been connected with the Théâtre Alfred Jarry. But this liaison too had ended when he discovered that she – 'my so-called wife' – had deceived him. In 1933 he met Anais Nin who was studying psychoanalysis with Dr Allendy and fell in love with her. In her diary for March 1933 Anais Nin gives a vivid picture of Artaud at this period of his life:

Artaud. Lean, taut. A gaunt face with visionary eyes. A sardonic manner. Now weary, now fiery and malicious. The theatre, for him, is a place to shout pain, anger, hatred, to enact the violence in us . . . He is the drugged, contracted being who walks always alone, who is seeking to produce plays which are like scenes of torture. His eyes are blue with languor, black with pain. He is all nerves. Yet he was beautiful acting the monk in love with Joan of Arc in the Carl Dreyer film. The deep-set eyes of the mystic, as if shining from caverns. Deep-set, shadowy, mysterious . . . Allendy had told me that he had tried to free Artaud of the drug habit which was destroying him. All I could see that evening was his revolt against interpretations. He was impatient with their presence, as if they prevented him from exaltation. He talked with fire about the Kabala, magic, myths, legends . . .⁴

Artaud, who at that time was writing his book on Heliogabalus, wrote Anais Nin long love letters. She noted in her diary (May 1933): 'Such an immense pity I have for Artaud, because he is always suffering . . . Physically I could not touch him, but the flame and genius in him I love'.⁵

In June 1933 Anais Nin met Artaud in a café. He asked her: 'People think I am mad. Do you think I am mad? Is that what frightens you?' She goes on: 'I knew at that moment, by his eyes, that he was, and that I loved his madness. I looked at his mouth, with the edges darkened by laudanum, a mouth I did not want to kiss. To be kissed by Artaud was to be drawn towards death, towards insanity . . .'⁶ 'Artaud' Anais Nin continues,

sat in the Coupole, pouring out poetry, talking of magic. 'I am Heliogabalus, the mad Roman emperor,' because he becomes everything he writes about. In the taxi he pushed back his hair from his ravaged face. The beauty of the summer day did not touch him. He stood up in the taxi and, stretching out his arms, he pointed to the crowded streets: 'The revolution will come soon. All this will be destroyed. The world must be destroyed. It is corrupt and full of ugliness. It is full of mummies, I tell you. Roman decadence. Death. I wanted a theatre that would be like a shock treatment, galvanize, shock people into feeling.' For the first time it seemed to me that Artaud was living in such a fantasy world that it was for himself he wanted a violent shock, to feel the reality of it, or the incarnating power of a great passion. But as he stood and shouted and spat with fury, the crowd stared at him and the taxi driver became nervous . . .[7]

Heliogabalus (*Héliogabale ou L'Anarchiste Couronné*) is a strange book. If Artaud's identification with the Roman emperor is to be believed – and there are a number of critics who regard the book as autobiographical in a deeper sense – his concept of his own life as an incarnation of ideas that could not be expressed in words alone would have been powerfully confirmed. He saw Heliogabalus, a homosexual who wanted to be a woman and was yet the priest of the masculine principle, the incarnation of the Sun as well as the Moon, as 'the paradigmatic image of this kind of dissociation of principles; the most clearly visible image of religious mania, of perversity and lucid folly, the image of all human contradictions . . .' (*OCVIII, 74-5*).

During 1934 Artaud had some further roles in films: in the summer of that year he went to southern Algeria to play the part of the Emir Abd-el-Kader in a musical based on an operetta about the conquest of Algeria in the 1840s, *Sidonie Panache*, produced by his cousin Alex Nalpas. The comedian Bach played the lead, while Artaud rolled his eyes and fumed as the villain of the piece. Another historical figure he portrayed was Savonarola in Abel Gance's *Lucrèce Borgia*. Fritz Lang gave him a part in an adaptation of Molnár's *Liliom* and Maurice Tourneur put him into another historical epic *Koenigsmarck*.

By February 1935 the manuscript of *The Cenci* was ready. Artaud gave a reading of it at the home of Jean-Marie Conty. The play, a four-act tragedy in prose, was full of blood and thunder, rape, incest and murder. Francesco Cenci is a historical figure, a Roman Renaissance aristocrat who had figured in a number of famous and scandalous cases before the papal courts. He raped his own daughter, Beatrice, and was murdered, allegedly on the instigation of the victim of the rape, Beatrice, together with his wife, Lucrezia. Stendhal had published an account of the affair, closely based on the actual trial records. And Shelley had written a five-act verse tragedy about it. Artaud's play is mainly based on Shelley's text, somewhat shortened and re-worked. The mad Count, who rapes his daughter not so much for lust but because he wants to condemn her to eternal damnation through incest, clearly was a tremendous part; and so was that of Beatrice, the innocent victim roused to take bloody vengeance and then condemned to death.

Fortunately, or unfortunately, for Artaud there was an actress interested in just such a part: an aristocratic lady with strong financial backing in Paris society: Iya Abdy, a delicate blonde beauty of Russian origin who had become Lady Abdy when she married Sir Robert Henry Edward Abdy, the fifth baronet of that name, whom, however, she had divorced in 1928 after five years of marriage. Lady Abdy had little experience of the stage, but she wanted to become an actress. She and Robert Denoel, the publisher of some of Artaud's writings, found the financial backing for a production of *The Cenci* as the first venture of Artaud's Theatre of Cruelty.

At last Artaud had an opportunity to realise at least some of his ambitions, although he insisted that this first production could by no means be regarded as a full embodiment of his theories. But it was a first step.

Much of Artaud's preparatory work in mounting *The Cenci* was inspired and original. But he also made some grave mistakes. Foremost among these was the choice of the venue for the experiment: the only theatre readily available was the Théâtre des Folies-Wagram (later re-named Théâtre de l'Etoile), built as the name implies as a music hall, a large cavernous place, surrounded by a *promenoir* and approached through a narrow corridor-like foyer. Although this was clearly most unsuitable and constituted a grave handicap for the production, Artaud decided to take it. He would use the foyer for an exhibition about the Balinese theatre and everything would work out fine.

André Frank, who acted as administrator for the enterprise, has described the period of rehearsals. Many of the actors did not grasp Artaud's new and original ideas. And 'if his views on the theatre were astonishing in their rigour and richness, his actual work in the theatre, however, was far removed from the expected. Perhaps the gap that had to be bridged between the theatre as it then was and the so-called Theatre of Cruelty was too large; he was many years ahead of the time for it'.[8] Artaud sensed all this. He became nervous and his nervousness transmitted itself to the actors. Some of them greatly profited by working for Artaud, chief among them Roger Blin, who acted as production assistant and played one of the two deaf-and-dumb murderers; he became one of Artaud's most loyal friends during the years of his confinement and was destined to emerge as one of the major figures of the post-war avantgarde theatre, a pioneer for the work of Adamov and Beckett. Jean-Louis Barrault who was assisting him with the production had been cast by Artaud as Beatrice's young brother, Bernardo. He participated in some of the rehearsals, but later dropped out, according to some sources because Dullin had refused to release him from his commitments at the *Atelier*, according to others because he had quarrelled with the star, Lady Abdy.

If the situation among the actors was not entirely happy, Artaud had shown immense flair in choosing his other collaborators. The great painter Balthus, whom Artaud deeply admired, agreed to design the scenery and costumes, and Roger Désormière composed the music, using up-to-date instruments like the Ondes Martenot. Artaud, who was convinced of the importance of sound in a production was also in advance of his time in the use of pre-recorded natural sounds coming stereophonically from loudspeakers placed in the auditorium: the bells of a cathedral (according to some Amiens, according to others Chartres) were used to great effect, as was real thunder, the noise of machinery, etc.

The opening night, a gala performance under the patronage of H.R.H. Princess George of Greece, the Princesse de Polignac and other society leaders in aid of the *Cercle François Villon*, was on 6 May 1935. The elegant establishment figures mingled with intellectuals in their berets and made the ugly old theatre with its hideously tasteless decoration vibrate with a degree of excitement. The reception seemed enthusiastic. But the reviews in the press were, on the whole, unfavourable. Far from being avantgarde, the melodramatic tragedy struck some critics as old-fashioned romantic fustian. And Lady Abdy, while admired for her grace and austere beauty, was savaged for her Russian accent and inaudible delivery. Others felt that Artaud would have been wiser to entrust the leading role to an actor less extreme and exaggerated than himself. He was accused of shouting his lines in paroxysms of intensity.

All now depended on the box-office. Would the public come? They did not. The play had to close, after seventeen performances, on 22 May 1935.

For Artaud it was a catastrophe. This had been his last chance to establish himself as a working director in the theatre of Paris. It had failed. No one would ever again be prepared to let him realise what were regarded as his extravagant and impractical ideas. This was more than merely a flop from which one could recover. It was, in effect, the end of Artaud's struggle since the early nineteen twenties to find a basis for a normal existence within the framework of society as it was constituted. André Frank has movingly recalled Artaud during the last days of the run of *The Cenci* when he first became aware of the significance of his failure:

I remember a terrible evening in the theatre, when Antonin Artaud for the first time showed the cramped, 'remote' face, cut off from the world, which has become the face by which we know him today. A financial failure, a chain of incomprehensions, had decided his fate: Artaud, the tragic genius, Artaud the prophet and magus, had come into existence.[9]

Jean-Louis Barrault offered Artaud the chance of collaborating with him on one of his theatrical ventures. But Artaud knew that it was too late. He declined the offer: 'I no longer believe in being associated with others, particularly since my experience with Surrealism, because I no longer believe in the purity of mankind ...' (*OCV*, 262).

What was he to do? He realised that he had reached the end of one road. There would have to be something like a new beginning. As far back as February he had suggested to Paulhan that the *NRF* should publish a volume of his collected writings on the theatre. Yet there was clearly no chance of his making a living as a writer. He had had some success as a lecturer at the Sorbonne. Perhaps he could lecture abroad. Filled with disgust as he was at the corruption of French, and European, society and art, yearning as he was for the freshness and purity of extra-European cultures, Balinese, Chinese, Tibetan he decided to try and leave Europe. His health, in spite of repeated attempts to cure himself of addiction, had been undermined by years of drug-taking. He wanted to abandon drugs and yet was passionately interested in them. Having worked on a project to dramatise the Spanish conquest of Mexico he had become aware of the existence of a mystical cult based on drugs there. All these considerations finally added up to the idea that he should go to Mexico as an apostle of French culture and, once there, study the remains of pre-Columbian culture and the cult of peyotl.

Through Paulhan, who had contacts at the Quai d'Orsay, Artaud eventually succeeded in obtaining some sort of official approval for his trip – a *titre de mission* – from the French Ministry of Education. Although this was little more than a formal endorsement, without any implications of financial subsidy, it at least had an effect on the Mexican Legation in Paris, which also gave its blessing. And as a result there was a chance that invitations to lecture and commissions for articles would be forthcoming once Artaud reached Mexico. To get there he had to borrow from his friends : Barrault, Lise Deharme, Paulhan and others advanced him some money and the Compagnie Transatlantique agreed to give him a fifty per cent reduction on his fare.

The last months of 1935 were spent in preparing this adventure. In the late autumn, shortly before his departure, Artaud met a young Belgian girl, Cécile Schramme, and fell deeply in love with her. She made him yearn for health and appeared in some ways as an embodiment of his dream of a return to a more normal existence. And as the day of his departure drew nearer he was also putting the finishing touches to the collection of essays about the theatre which the *NRF* had undertaken to publish. Three days before he left Paris for Antwerp, on 6 January 1936 he sent Paulhan the suggested order in which the essays should be published. No title had yet been chosen for the book. It was during the sea voyage from Antwerp to Havana that he finally decided on a title and wrote to Paulhan about it: 'I think I have found a suitable title for my book. It will be THE THEATRE AND ITS DOUBLE. For if the theatre is a double of life, life is a double of true theatre. . . . The double of the theatre is the *reality* which today's mankind leaves unused' (*OCV*, 272-3).

The S.S. *Albertville* had sailed from Antwerp on 10 January and arrived in Havana on 30 January 1936. It was Artaud's first glimpse of the New World. And here there happened something to which he later attached immense, cosmic importance: in circumstances which he regarded as mysterious and fateful he somehow obtained a small dagger or replica of a sword, a Toledan blade. It had, he maintained, been given him by a Negro sorcerer as a gift. He looked upon it as a powerful omen of good fortune to come.

On 7 February 1936 he disembarked on Mexican soil at Veracruz and took the train to Mexico City.

In Mexico he was well received as a prominent Frenchman, an established figure of Parisian cultural life who could speak with authority about the latest developments in the world's artistic capital. He was lionised, invited to lunch by the French Minister, commissioned to write a series of articles for an important newspaper *El Nacional Revolucionario*, and invited to lecture at various institutions of higher learning.

Yet it was not all smooth sailing. He was in constant financial trouble. And he managed to offend some powerful circles. The Communist Party, an important force in Mexican politics at the time, took umbrage at his disparaging remarks about the political commitment of the Surrealists. Nor was his insistence on the inherent superiority of ancient Indian culture over the corrupt civilisation of Europe wholly welcome to a regime which was desperately trying to drag Mexico into an industrial, twentieth-century way of life.

In spite of all this, he succeeded eventually in obtaining, with the help of the Rector of Mexico University, financial assistance for a visit to an area inhabited by hitherto unspoilt Indian tribes to study their art.

It was at the end of August 1936 that he set out, by train, to cover the eight hundred miles to Shihuahua. From there, riding on a horse, he travelled into the Sierra Madre and into the country inhabited by the Tarahumara tribe, the Sierra Tarahumara. If we are to believe the description he gave of this ride after his return to Paris, it was a most painful journey: two men had to lift him on and off the horse, so helpless and sick was Artaud; they had to put the reins into his hands and even close them around the reins, as he was unable to control his own movements. Perhaps this state of enfeeblement was due to the fact that he had abandoned the use of drugs in order to prepare his body to receive the peyotl. During the ride he had the impression that the rock formations resembled either the image of a dying man or female breasts and he felt compelled to count the rocks, only to find that they recurred with miraculous regularity in groups of 3, 4, 7 and 8. He was reminded of the music of numbers in the Cabbala.

When he arrived in the country of the Tarahumara, Artaud, who carried a letter from the Ministry of Education, was housed in the local school. The teacher aroused Artaud's dislike by obviously being eager to stamp out the last vestiges of the native religion; but also by being mainly preoccupied with fornicating with his female colleague. It was only after lengthy arguments that Artaud finally persuaded the teacher to allow the village priests to perform their ritual. He also apparently succeeded in obtaining some peyotl. After his return to Paris he recorded that it made him think 'then, at that moment, that I was living through the happiest three days of my existence. I had ceased to be bored, to seek a reason for my existence, and I ceased to have to carry my body. I understood that I invented life, and that *that* was my function and my *raison d'être* and that I was bored when I no longer had my imagination and that the peyotl gave me imagination' (*OCIX*, 117).

By 7 October Artaud was back in Chihuahua and anxiously inquired from Paulhan whether *The Theatre and its Double* had yet appeared. He also announced that he was about to return to France. On 31 October 1936 he embarked on the *Mexique* and arrived back in France at St Nazaire on 12 November.

The flight to the New World had proved a failure. It had not provided Artaud with a basis for an ordered existence. Back in Paris he was destitute, ravaged by drug addiction, without visible means of support. Jean-Marie Conty allowed him to stay in his house. Paulhan promised to publish his account of his journey into the land of the Tarahumara. Other friends helped him out with money. He met Cécile Schramme again, the Belgian girl who had so deeply impressed him before his departure for Mexico. His love letters to her between January and May 1937 give a pathetic picture of deep affection and a dream of married happiness, but also of continuous quarrels: Artaud wanted to reach the pinnacle of spiritual, non-sexual love and reproached Cécile with secret relapses into the common ways of female sexual greed. At the same time Artaud was resolved to purge himself of the drug habit. A grant of 600 francs, as an emergency subsidy, from the Ministry of Education's *Caisse des Lettres* enabled him to undergo a disintoxication treatment (25 February to 4 March 1937) at the Centre Français de Médecine et de Chirurgie in the Rue Boileau. But this did not succeed in ridding him of the after-effects of long years of addiction to laudanum, opium and heroin. From 14 to 29 April he made another effort, this time in a clinic at Sceaux. After this he felt much changed and able to meet his fiancée's parents, respectable bourgeois of Brussels. On 18 May 1937 he was to deliver a lecture on the crisis of the cultural life of Paris, as seen by a traveller recently returned from Mexico, at the Brussels Maison de l'Art. It is difficult now to establish what actually happened at this occasion; it certainly ended in scandal. According to one account, Artaud announced that he would not be talking about the advertised subject and would instead give an account of his travels to the Tarahumara. As he was talking his attitude towards the audience became more and more aggressive and he ended with a furious shriek: 'In revealing all this to you, I have probably killed myself'. After which he remained motionless, with his eyes closed. According to rumours circulating in Brussels at the time, however, Artaud had shocked his audience by talking, instead of his advertised subject, 'on the effects of masturbation on the Jesuits'. While this is itself improbable, it shows the impression his behaviour had made on at least some members of his audience.

On 21 May, back in Paris, Artaud was still writing to Paulhan asking him to act as best man at his marriage to Cécile Schramme. But, in fact, the engagement was already off. Cécile's parents, with whom Artaud had stayed at Brussels, were scandalised and far from satisfied that the strange Paris Bohemian was a suitable husband for their daughter. Later Artaud bitterly complained that Cécile herself had been spreading calumnies about him, telling people that he was subject to fits of madness.

The disaster of the trip to Brussels was another turning point. Artaud became convinced that his very name had to disappear, an indication that he felt that his entire previous existence had collapsed. He begged Paulhan, at the beginning of June 1937, to publish his account of his trip to the Tarahumara anonymously, with merely three asterisks in place of the author's name. 'Very soon I shall be dead or else in a situation . . . in which I shall not need a name. I am counting on you for the three asterisks' (*OCVII*, 227). The change he was expecting to undergo was connected with his increased preoccupation with magic and miraculous signs surrounding him. One of these was the mysterious little sword in Toledan steel that he had received from a Negro sorcerer in Havana. But even more powerful and fateful was an Irish walking stick which his friend René Thomas had given him, and of which it was said that it might have belonged to St Patrick himself, being perhaps the very stick with which he banished all snakes from Ireland. Artaud, in any case, later maintained that this walking stick 'which everybody has been able to see in Paris in May, June, July and August 1937' had been given to René Thomas by 'the daughter of a Savoyard magician' (*OCIX*, 195). This cane had 13 knobs or knots and Artaud was convinced that this was the identical number of knots on St Patrick's stick of which, he remembered, he had read in a dictionary of hagiography he had consulted in the Bibliothèque Nationale in 1934 when researching his book on Heliogabalus.

To fathom the significance of all these magical events Artaud was taking lessons in the interpretation of the tarot pack. In June 1937 he experienced illumination. And as a result he published, at the end of July, a brochure, without an author's name and merely signed *Le Révélé* (The Revealed One), *Les Nouvelles Révélations de l'Etre* (The New Revelations of Being) in which he prophesied the forthcoming destruction of civilisation by Fire, Water, Earth and 'a Star which will occupy the entire surface of the air, in which the Spirit of Man had been immersed' (*OCVII*, 173). It is a strange work, filled with numerological calculations and tarot interpretations, yet imbued with a powerful, poetic impetus of divine fury. It is also a declaration to the world, that the author has reached a state of final separation from normal existence:

> I have struggled to try and exist, to try and consent to the forms (all the forms) with which the delirious illusion of being in the world has imbued reality.

> I no longer want to be deceived by illusions.
> Dead for the world; to that which for all others constitutes the world; fallen at last, fallen, risen into the void which I had rejected. I have a body which experiences the world and spews out reality.

> . . . .

> He who is speaking to you is one who has truly despaired and who has known the happiness of being in the world only now when he has left the world, when he is absolutely separated from it.

> Being dead, the others are not separated. They are still circling around their own corpses.

> I am not dead. But I am separated. (*OCVII, 150-1*)

The miraculous little sword and the cane are variously referred to in the book: 'I have the sword from an African Negro; the cane I have from God' (*OCVII, 163*). The male and female principle play a considerable part. One cycle of the world's history is approaching its end; it was dominated by the female principle, which stands for the Left, Republic and Democracy. This means that the masses will again fall under the yoke. They deserve it. And through whom is this cosmic change to happen? 'Through a Madman who is also a Sage and who sees himself as both Sage and Madman.' This image recurs in various guises through the tarot symbols. 'The tortured man has been taken for a Madman by everybody. He has appeared before the world as a Madman. And the image of the world's madness was incarnated in a tortured man' (*OCVII, 170*). And that Artaud saw himself as the tortured man becomes clear at the end of the pamphlet in which he predicts the holocaust for November 1937:

> On the 7th (of November) the Destruction explodes in Lightning. The Tortured Man becomes, for the whole

World, the Recognised One,
          The Revealed One. (*OCVII*, 174)

In thus signing the pamphlet Artaud reveals *himself* as the tortured bringer of destruction – and through destruction, salvation – to the world.

Convinced that destiny called him to a cosmic event, Artaud felt that he had to be in the right place when it occurred. And that right place was the country where his miraculous walking stick had come from – the West of Ireland, the country of St Patrick.

So, following the same instinct that had driven him to Mexico, but in a state far less lucid, far more exalted, Artaud prepared himself for another journey into the unknown. Having lost Cécile Schramme he developed new fervent attachments to women; he saw a mystic bond between himself and Jacqueline Breton, André Breton's daughter. (After his return from Mexico he had renewed his old friendship with Breton and buried the old clamorous feuds with him.) Another woman who began to play an important part in his life and to whom he addressed passionate letters was Anne Manson, a young journalist who, planning a trip to Mexico, had been advised to contact Artaud. It was to these women he poured out his visions, warning them of the dangers of future destruction and promising them his protection. And his behaviour became ever more strange. In August 1937 Anaïs Nin noted in her diary: 'The Dôme at nine in the morning. Antonin Artaud passes by. He is waving his magic Mexican cane and shouting'.[10]

On 14 August Artaud sent his first postcards from Ireland to René Thomas, who had given him the magic cane (which Anaïs Nin had, understandably, mistaken for a Mexican object), his sister and André Breton. He had arrived at Cobh. On 17 August he was in Galway. On 23 August he wrote to Anne Manson from the island of Inishmore in the Aran Islands, where he had found lodgings in a remote village, more than two hours' walk from the nearest post office at Kilronan. He had run out of money by then and was asking Breton and Paulhan to help him. On 2 September he left the island (without apparently paying his bill at the place where he had stayed) and went to Galway where he took lodgings at the Imperial Hotel. A letter he wrote to Breton from there

on 5 September was, he declared, the last he would ever
sign with his name; henceforth he would be known by another name. On 8 September he left Galway, apparently for
Dublin. As the hour of the catastrophe he had foreseen
for the world approached, the miraculous cane changed
character: on 14 September he wrote to Anne Manson: 'I
hold Jesus Christ's own baton and it is Jesus Christ who
commands me, and all that I shall do; and it will be seen
that His teaching was for Metaphysical Heroes and not for
idiots' (*OCVII*, 282). But in a letter to Breton written on the
same day he made it clear that the Jesus Christ whose cane
he possessed had nothing to do with the Jesus Christ of
Christianity. If the Holy Ghost was a force urging men to
live, it was Artaud's Christ-Shiva who called men towards
the Absolute, because he recognised that Life is Evil and
Death the ultimate Good.

What actually happened to Artaud in Dublin in the second
half of September 1937 remains shrouded in mystery. The
most probable version is that, completely without money
and in considerable distress, he tried to make contact with
some religious house which he thought might contain French-
speaking monks. It is said that, having tried to gain access
to a monastery (or perhaps even a convent) late at night and
not getting anyone to open the door, he made such a noise
in the street, that the police were called to put an end to
the disturbance. As he resisted being moved on, there was
a scuffle in which the miraculous cane of St Patrick was lost.
He spent six days in detention and was finally put on a ship
bound for Le Havre, the S.S. *Washington*, which left Cobh
on 29 September 1937.

Worse was to come. Having been assigned a cabin on board
the *Washington*, Artaud, it seems, was alarmed by the
sudden appearance of a steward and a mechanic, carrying
metal implements, probably in order to repair a washbasin.
Convinced that the two sinister figures had come to harm
him, Artaud furiously attacked them and had to be overpowered and put into a strait-jacket. On arrival at Le Havre
on 30 September 1937 the owners of the ship handed him
over to the French authorities, who promptly interned him
in an asylum as a dangerous lunatic. It was the beginning of
nine long years of confinement in mental institutions.

Artaud had predicted the ultimate catastrophe for November 1957. As far as the ultimate catastrophe for himself was concerned, his margin of error amounted to barely more than a month. And as regards the whole world's holocaust – the outbreak of the Second World War – that occurred within less than two years of the predicted date. Detained first in Le Havre itself, then transferred to the asylum of Quatre-Mares at Sotteville-lès-Rouen. Artaud had disappeared from the view of all his friends. Artaud's mother had been notified of her son's internment by the shipping line, but had some difficulty in discovering his whereabouts. She finally traced him to Quatre-Mares but he was unable to recognise her. Whatever his mental state might have been at the moment, when, unable to communicate in a world which did not speak his language, he had suddenly been overpowered and detained, the shock of this sudden incarceration would, in itself, more than account for his having fallen into an almost catatonic state.

His family desperately tried to have him freed, or at least moved nearer to Paris, where it would be easier to visit him. On 12 April 1938 these efforts resulted in his transfer to the mental hospital of Sainte-Anne in Paris. Here some of his friends were able to gain access to him, but he hardly responded. In fact, the authorities came to the conclusion that he was incurable; he was accordingly transferred to an institution for such cases, the mental hospital of Ville-Evrard on the outskirts of Paris, on 27 February 1939.

It is ironical that, at the very moment when Artaud was in a near-catatonic state in the hospital of Sainte-Anne, the book through which he is still exercising a deep influence on the development of the theatre, *The Theatre and its Double*, was finally published. He had collected the articles and essays it contains before his departure to Mexico, had begged Paulhan to speed its publication before leaving for Ireland and had asked for an advance for it while penniless in the Isles of Aran. At last, in February 1938, it appeared in the Gallimard series *Métamorphoses* in an edition limited to four hundred copies – and its author was not even aware of it.

Yet the publication had drawn attention to Artaud and interest in him re-awakened among the intellectuals of Paris. From Ville-Evrard Artaud also began to remind his friends of his existence. He started writing letters and agreed to see visitors. 'I am a fanatic, I am not a madman' he wrote to

Jacqueline Breton on 7 April 1939. To Roger Blin and Charles Dullin he addressed moving appeals to rescue him from confinement. At the end of 1940 he began to write again to Genica Athanasiou, the companion of his early years in Paris. He knew, he said, that she had fought valiantly in the battles conducted by his friends for his release. (He later told Breton that tens of thousands had filled the streets of Le Havre demanding his release at the moment of his arrest and that Breton had, in fact, been killed during the ensuing massacre.) 'Heroin must be procured at all costs and it must be brought to me even at the risk of getting killed. . . . The initiates have real instruments of torture, as I have told you, and they use them from afar to mutilate me a little more every night while I am asleep, . . .' he wrote to Genica on 24 November 1940, '. . . Genica, we must leave this world, but to be able to do that, the Reign of the Other World must come, and for that armed troops in great numbers are needed. So that the Bohemians can enter *in numbers* into this world, as one passes from a ship to the quayside, I need heroin to open the hidden doors for them and to break the spells of Satan which keep them out and me prisoner here.'[11]

There is no doubt that Artaud's rage at being confined also led him into violent fantasies of persecution. According to Jean-Louis Brau a series of letters written by Artaud to one of the doctors at the asylum, which are extant, cannot as yet be published because of the most terrible accusations they contain against persons who are still alive.

As time passed and Artaud remained at Ville-Evrard, the situation became more and more dangerous for him. France, by then, was under German occupation, there was a severe shortage of food; the inmates of lunatic asylums were at the very bottom of the list of priorities. Moreover it was known that, in Germany itself, lunatics and mental defectives had been liquidated by the authorities to save food supplies. Artaud's mother and those of his friends who occasionally visited him were appalled by his loss of weight and his emaciated state.

Desnos, Eluard, Barrault, Theodore Fraenkel and Arthur Adamov were trying to think of ways and means to save Artaud. Mme Bourdet, a cousin of Adamov's, had been impressed by the humanity and openness of mind of a psychiatrist, Dr Gaston Ferdière, whom she had met while he was in charge of an institution near where she lived and who had since then become head of a mental hospital in the south of France, in the zone then still unoccupied by the Germans, where conditions were much easier. Ferdière, himself a poet and essayist of some note, had frequented the intellectual circles where Artaud had moved in the thirties and may even have met him occasionally. He was certainly aware of Artaud's stature as a poet and man of the theatre. When Desnos approached Ferdière in November 1942, he readily agreed to do his best for Artaud, and to take him into his institution at Rodez in the department of Aveyron, some 100 miles north-east of Toulouse. But to transfer a mental patient across the zonal borders was far from easy. Ferdière hit upon a solution: Desnos and Artaud's family would ask for his transfer to another institution *within* the German zone of occupation, but very near the demarcation line, the 'rural' mental asylum at Chézal-Benoît, of which Ferdière had previously been the médical director, and where he still had friends willing to help him. From there it would be easier to move Artaud across the demarcation line. Desnos managed to obtain permission to have Artaud moved from Ville-Evrard in January 1943. On the eve of his departure he went to visit him, and, not having seen him for five years, was horrified to find him emaciated and in a state of delirium: '. . . talking like St Jerome and unwilling to leave because it might remove him from the magical powers at work for him'.[12] Nevertheless Desnos persuaded Artaud's mother to give her permission to have her son moved.

Artaud left Ville-Evrard on 22 January and, after spending three weeks at Chézal-Benoît, arrived at Rodez in the early morning of 11 February 1943. Ferdière went to meet Artaud at the station. He was, so he later said, determined from the beginning to treat him with the respect due to a great poet, however sick he might be. Artaud declared himself happy to meet him again and although Ferdière, who had seen him from the distance, could not remember actually having been introduced to him, he readily responded. ' I said, "Yes, certainly I remember, I'm glad you've come here" and very soon I was treating Artaud not as a sick man withdrawn from the world but as someone I knew intimately; and I tried to restore to him the quality of human dignity of which he had been so long deprived. My wife helped me to play this little game . . . so when we arrived at Rodez, she immediately invited him to lunch'.[13] Frédéric Delanglade, a painter who was a friend of Ferdière's, was present at this lunch. Artaud, when introduced by his name, retorted: 'Antonin Artaud is dead, my name is Antonin Nalpas'.[14] Until September 1943 he continued to sign his letters with that – his mother's maiden-name.

Although Artaud behaved extremely strangely, uttering wild cries and circling about the room, Ferdière treated him as a friend, gave him a small room of his own and, as the Aveyron department was in a fertile region and had a flourishing black market, fattened him up with milk, honey, biscuits and other foods he had not tasted for years.

When he arrived at Rodez Artaud had already spent almost five and a half years in mental institutions. At Rodez he began a copious correspondence with numerous old friends and acquaintances and also wrote long letters to the doctors at Rodez. These reveal that he had become extremely pious and eager to attend church services. He attributed his internment to the machinations of the Anti-Christ and his agents, the French police who were in league with the Jews, and other sinister forces of evil. They had poisoned him and were keeping from him the only antidote to the poison from which he suffered – and that antidote was opium. The poison which was the cause of Artaud's torments, however, was sperm, obtained by the police by putting vast crowds of people under erotic spells which induced them into ritual masturbation.

> All sexuality and all eroticism. . . . are a sin and a crime against Jesus Christ and the antidote to eroticism and the spells of the Demon is opium and it is to prevent me from taking opium and to leave me as a target for the erotic manoeuvres of the demons against me that the French police, which entirely belongs to the Antichrist, is keeping me prisoner. To cure me of Evil I need opium and to refuse me opium amounts to becoming an accomplice of the Demons (*OCX*, 16).

Antonin Artaud, he claimed in another letter, had died at Ville-Evrard in August 1939; it was merely his body which had remained as a vessel into which God would descend when it was duly purified (*OCX*, 40). In a letter to Paulhan, dated 7 July 1943, he spoke of Saint-Artaud who had dominated vast crowds, trying to prevent him from going to Ireland, by striking lightning from St Patrick's cane outside the offices of the *NRF* in the Rue Sébastien Bottin; and that he had gone to Ireland to return the sacred cane of St Patrick to St Patrick's Cathedral in Dublin where it had been attached to a wall for 1500 years until it disappeared in the nineteenth century; and that, while in Dublin he had also ascertained that the Holy Grail, which had been brought to Ireland by King Cormac Mac Art was still there. And if Antonin Artaud had led a double life, so did Jean Paulhan who was also known in Paradise and among the Saints as Dionysos the Aeropagite (*OCX*, 57-9). The idea that several different souls could successively inhabit the same body dominated much of Artaud's thought at this period. Of friends who somehow disappointed him he maintained that they had died, while some demon continued to inhabit their bodies and deceived all those with whom they came into contact that they were still alive.

Another dominant idea of his fantasies at this time was the utter wickedness of all sexuality. In a long letter to one of the doctors at Rodez Artaud demonstrated that God had created Man without the need of sexual reproduction or defecation; originally Man possessed neither sexual nor digestive organs, food was originally eliminated by 'lumbar evaporation'. It was Anti-Christ who had seduced man into the filthy habits of coition and digestion (*OCX*, 31-5).

The body of Antonin Artaud had, he asserted again and again, carried all the world's sins and impurities; that was the reason for his intense suffering. Artaud's soul, on the other hand, he told Jean-Louis Barrault in one of his early letters from Rodez, was that of an angel who had previously dwelt on earth under the name of St Hyppolitus, Bishop of Piraeus in the second century AD (*OCX*, 40). Yet he frequently heard other people converse within his own body, he told Frédéric Delanglade, 'because my thoughts are pure, and, when I have a bad thought, I never believe that it is my own and immediately try to discover the impure consciousness which has sent it to soil me' (*OCX*, 52).

Dr Ferdière tried to stimulate Artaud into activity, encouraging him to draw, lending him books and, later, suggesting that he should make translations from the English. In the course of 1944 Artaud translated Robert Southwell's *The Burning Babe* which Pierre Seghers published in *Poésie 44*, Edgar Allan Poe's *Israfel* and Lewis Carroll's *Ye Carpette Knight* (although Artaud had always detested Lewis Carroll). As early as the autumn of 1943 a publisher, Robert J. Godet, approached Artaud for permission to publish the texts about his voyage to Mexico, which had appeared in the *NRF* before the war, as an illustrated book. Perdière encouraged Artaud to write additional material about his Mexican adventure and Artaud immediately set to work on the first of several essays, which, although the original plan of publication came to nothing, eventually appeared in book form.

Occupational therapy, however, was not the only form of treatment Ferdière had in store for Artaud. He felt that Artaud was in danger of further deterioration and of a gradual but continuous slide into ever deeper alienation, delusion and eventual apathy. And so he decided to subject him to several courses of electric shock treatment. For Artaud this amounted to sheer torture and later it was to become the subject of bitter accusations against Ferdière by Artaud and his supporters. For although, as Ferdière never tired of pointing out, the actual treatment is painless, Artaud was filled with horror and fear of the moment, when, on regaining consciousness, the patient is at first unaware of his whereabouts and, indeed, his own identity. These moments of re-awakening into a void caused Artaud profound existential anguish. By July 1945, after two years at Rodez, Artaud maintained that he had been through no less than fifty such comas (*OCX, 93*). On the other hand, Ferdière claimed that the electric shock treatment was greatly improving Artaud's behaviour and was dispelling his obsessions and delusions. There were certainly indications of an improvement in Artaud's state of mind. In a letter, addressed to one of the doctors at Rodez who had been against continuing his electric shock treatment, Artaud pleaded with him to stop any further such torture, on the grounds that 'I no longer believe in the démons of hell as I did two years ago when I arrived here . . . And as I don't want to think of these any more I have, for quite a long time now, stopped seeing anything but the paper on which I am writing, the people, the trees, the houses among which I live and the blue sky above' (*OCXI, 14*). Was this new attitude – from which Artaud quite soon relapsed into further accusations against 'initiates' who were poisoning him and keeping him under their spell – the result of the treatment? Or did it merely show that in his fear of further torture Artaud was prepared to assert anything which he believed might convince his tormentors that he no longer needed electric shock treatment?

Be that as it may, by the spring of 1945 Artaud had emerged from his lengthy period of religious fervour. It was, he told Blin in a letter, in April, on Passion Sunday, that he had 'thrown communion, the Eucharist, God and his Christ out of the window and I have decided to be myself, that is, simply Antonin Artaud, a religious unbeliever by nature and soul who has never hated anything more than God and his religions, whether that of Christ or Jehovah or Brahma, not forgetting the naturist rites of the lamas' (*OCXI*, 29). Yet in the same letter he insisted that he was under more spells than ever and that the Sûreté Générale, the British Intelligence service and the Vatican's Congregation of the Index were plotting against him.

In May 1944 *The Theatre and its Double* had been re-issued by Gallimard. And after the liberation of Paris in August of that year, as the literary life gradually returned to normality, Artaud was able to resume contact with his former literary circle, as well as a new generation for whom he had become something of a legendary, martyred figure. He was greatly touched when a young writer and critic, Henri Thomas, who was writing an essay on *The Theatre and its Double*, approached him in January 1945 with a request for personal information and permission to visit him. Ironically, at that time, Artaud himself had not yet seen his book. When at last a copy of the new edition reached him at the end of January 1945, the first he had ever held in his hand, he wrote to Paulhan: 'My heart is deeply agitated to see so much dynamism, such forcefulness of style at the service of ideas which, in the face of the upheaval, the disorder, the anarchy and war of the present situation, no longer are directed at the points that should be aimed at' (*OCXI*, 29). By now Artaud was no longer confined within the asylum, he was able to go for walks around Rodez, a little town with a fine cathedral. And he received more and more visitors from Paris: Raymond Queneau had come to see him as early as Christmas 1943. After the end of the war Jean Dubuffet, Henri Thomas and others came to Rodez, were duly horrified by the dinginess of the asylum in its ancient building, and strolled through the town in deep conversation with Artaud.

Among the new friends with whom Artaud corresponded after the liberation was Henri Parisot, a young man who was trying to re-launch the project which had become bogged down, of a book about Artaud's visit to Mexico. When Parisot suggested that he might publish the five long letters he had received from Artaud in the autumn of 1945 and which gave an account of his views about the origins of his confinement, his drug addiction and language, poetry and art, Artaud agreed. When that little book, the *Letters from Rodez*, appeared in April 1946, Artaud was already on the eve of his departure.

Artaud's former friends and the growing number of new admirers had long been trying to free him from his confinement. Early in 1946 Marthe Robert, the translator of Kafka, and Arthur Adamov came to Rodez to negotiate with Dr Ferdière about Artaud's release. Ferdière agreed on condition that he should be satisfied that Artaud's livelihood was assured. Accordingly a committee was formed in Paris with the task of raising sufficient funds.

The committee's appeal for help found a most generous response. Artists like Picasso, Giacommetti, Duchamp, Braque, Arp, Léger, Masson, to name but a few of the most famous, donated works to be sold by auction, together with manuscripts and autographs provided by writers of the stature of Gide, Eluard, Mauriac, Sartre, René Char, Supervielle and Tzara; while Artaud's theatrical friends were planning a gala matinée with the participation of Barrault, Blin, Dullin, Jouvet, Alain Cuny and Jean Vilar. Ferdière was satisfied. He released Artaud from the asylum on 19 March 1946, but advised him to spend some time on his own in a village some 20 kilometres from Rodez. He returned to Rodez on 14 April and was accompanied by Ferdière himself to Paris on 26 May 1946.

On the platform of the Gare d'Austerlitz a group of Artaud's friends was waiting for the arrival of the night train from Rodez. The man they welcomed back to the city he had left almost nine years earlier was not yet fifty. But toothless, wrinkled, ravaged as he was, he looked well over seventy.

Ferdière had recommended that Artaud should remain under some psychiatric care. So his friends had arranged for him to lodge, as a purely voluntary patient, in an old pavilion in the garden of the psychiatric hospital at Ivry, on the outskirts of Paris, near the end-point of the metro-line which goes to the Mairie d'Ivry. Gérard de Nerval one of the *poètes maudits* with whom Artaud felt so much kinship, had been an inmate of that same institution and Artaud also maintained that some of the heroes of the French Revolution, Robespierre and Marat, had made speeches in the building.

The auction of works of art which opened with a *vernissage* at the Galerie Pierre (managed by Pierre Loeb) cn 6 June and the benefit performance at the Théâtre Sarah-Bernhardt at 5 p.m. on 7 June were a great success and realised the sum of about one million (post-war inflated) francs for Artaud. The matinée at the theatre was attended by *tout Paris*: Vilar, Cuny, Jouvet and Rouleau read from Artaud's works; Colette Thomas, Henri Thomas's wife, recited a recent poem she had rehearsed with Artaud himself; this was Artaud's authentic voice and the outstanding performance of the evening. Breton, Dullin, Adamov and Barrault spoke about Artaud. Then Barrault announced that there would be a reading from *The Cenci* lasting forty minutes. The young poet Jacques Prevel, one of those who had written to Artaud at Rodez, noted in his diary that Barrault gave a tremendous performance. Strangely enough, Barrault himself has subsequently denied any recollection of having taken part in this benefit performance, although his name is on the advertisement for it and although witnesses like Prevel have recorded the fact. The reason may well be that Barrault, who later became disgusted by the cult of Artaud in circles he disliked, simply does not want to remember.

Artaud himself was not present in the theatre. He waited at a café for the performance to end and then happily wandered off with Adamov.

Back in the familiar and yet now so different world of the cafés of St Germain-des-Prés, surrounded by old friends and new admirers, Artaud became immensely active: he who had had such difficulty in putting his thoughts on paper was now writing incessantly, day and night, at home, with friends in cafés, on the metro; the barriers which had stood between his thought and its expression and which he had so movingly described in the correspondence with Rivière had fallen, and when existing words failed him he inserted newly-formed words as yet without meaning or simply random groups of vowels and consonants which stood for inarticulate cries and murmurs.

Gallimard planned an edition of his complete works. For this he wrote a Preamble in which he affirmed that he had abandoned the search for perfect expression ('*Que mes phrases sonnent le français ou le papou, c'est exactment ce dont je me fous*' – Whether my sentences sound French or Papuan, that's exactly what I don't care a damn). He also added, as supplements to the letters he had written to the Pope and the Dalai Lama in his Surrealist period, new letters to these personages in which he used far more violent language and, indeed, as far as the Dalai Lama was concerned completely reversed his position. To the Pope he declared, among other things, that 'it was I (not Jesus Christ) who was crucified on Golgotha; and I was crucified for having risen against God and his Christ, because I am a man and God and his Christ are only ideas, which, incidentally, carry the filthy marks of the hands of man; and these ideas have never existed for me' (*OCI*, 17), while he accused the Dalai Lama and his like of being 'merely filthy Europeans, after all, as the real Orient was Nordic. . . . It is you who are the cause of the syllogism, of logic, of hysterical mysticism, of the dialectic . . .' (*OCI*, 23), to mention only a few of the crimes laid at his feet. While still in Rodez Artaud had planned a third mystical journey, this time to Tibet. Now, after his return to Paris, he was, as Prevel noted in his diary, thinking of it again. Speaking of the journey he planned to the Far East right into China, he said 'We'll go, fifty strong, armed with rifles and machine guns, and we'll settle some accounts with certain people, particularly in Tibet.'[15]

Many of Artaud's poems written at this time immediately appeared in reviews or were issued as expensive pamphlets.

At the end of 1946 Artaud decided that he wanted to give a public reading of some of his current work. It was arranged that this should take place on 13 January 1947 at the Théâtre du Vieux Colombier. He was to read three poems, *Le Retour d'Artaud le Mômo* [Mômo is Marseilles argot for a fool] among them. On 11 January he told Prevel that he was suffering from an eczema on his testicles, but that Dr Thévenin, the husband of Paule Thévenin, who had become Artaud's un-official secretary and helper (and later the editor of his collected works) had treated it and given him permission to appear.

The theatre was sold out. The *Letters from Rodez* had made Artaud well-known among the younger intellectuals. But older literary figures, like André Gide, were also in the audience. Artaud, as he had done at the disastrous lecture in Brussels which had spoiled his chances of marriage, soon abandoned his prepared programme and launched into an account of his sufferings at the hands of psychiatrists and of the horrors of electric shock treatment. Having dropped the papers with his prepared text, he went on talking for two hours; then his voice gave out. He stopped, and finally fled from the stage. André Gide felt that it was one of the most moving moments he had ever experienced: 'Of his material being nothing remained except what was expressive'.[16] But the paying customers on the whole felt let down and, to them, this appearance of Artaud in public, like so many previous ones, seemed nothing short of scandalous.

At about the same time, in January 1947, a great van Gogh exhibition was held at the Orangerie. Artaud went to see it and was overwhelmed by the work of a kindred spirit who had also languished in a lunatic asylum. When Pierre Loeb, the art dealer, a few days later showed Artaud an article in a newspaper which described van Gogh as a degenerate, Artaud became so incensed that he began writing an essay in defence of the painter. This, *Van Gogh, le suicidé de la société* (Van Gogh, 'suicided' by society) is one of Artaud's most brilliant and influential works. It was awarded the Prix St Beuve shortly after it appeared at the end of 1947. Apart from passages of splendid analysis and description of van Gogh's paintings, this essay is, above all, a furious polemic against psychiatrists and psychiatry. Part of it was published in an English translation by Peter Watson in the number of *Horizon* for January 1948. That is where R. D. Laing read it as a young student; he has since said that it came as a revelation to him and played a decisive part in his development.

In July 1947 Pierre Loeb arranged an exhibition of Artaud's drawings at his gallery and Artaud also gave a reading of his poems there.

With several publications of his poems imminent (*Artaud*

le Mômo and *Ci-gît*) Artaud was much in demand. In November 1947 Fernand Pouey, in charge of literary and dramatic broadcasts at the French Radio, asked Artaud to appear in a series called *La Voix des Poètes*. Using some of his writings which were already in existence (he asked Paule Thévenin, to take part and to choose which of his texts she wanted to read), Artaud dictated a good deal of new material, to form part of the broadcast which he called *Pour en finir avec le pugement de Dieu*. The transmission was rehearsed and recorded from 22 to 29 November 1947 in the studios of the Radiodiffusion Française. Apart from Artaud himself the speakers were Paule Thévenin, Roger Blin and Maria Casarès. Artaud himself accompanied some of the text on xylophone, drums, gongs and other percussion instruments which were put at his disposal. After the programme had been edited, in January 1948, Artaud made some cuts and even re-recorded part of it. The transmission was scheduled for 22.45 hrs on 2 February 1948. But on 1 February Wladimir Porché, the Director General of the Radiodiffusion Français, decided to stop the broadcast.

Artaud certainly had produced some inflammatory material. The first text which he spoke himself concerned a plan he imagined he had heard about, according to which the United States, afraid that they would be lacking cannon-fodder for future wars they had planned, were stockpiling the sperm of little boys about to enter school in deep-frozen form to be used in artificial insemination for the subsequent production of soldiers. In another passage God was called no more than shit and ridicule was heaped on the Mass as well as Jesus Christ. Pouey, the originator of the transmission, argued that had Rimbaud been alive he would probably have produced equally shocking material – and would posterity not have ridiculed broadcasting authorities that denied him the opportunity to be heard? The press was puzzled and outraged by the cancellation. As a result it was decided that the recording should be heard by a jury of prominent literary figures who could support Fernand Pouey in his resolve to have the programme broadcast. This audition took place on 5 February: among those who heard Artaud's poems were Raymond Queau, Max-Pol Fouchet, Cocteau, Roger Vitrac and other prominent personalities. They unanimously supported a broadcast. But the Director General remained adamant. Fernand Pouey resigned. The controversy in the press raged for many days. Again Artaud was at the centre of a scandal and a storm. It was the last time.

Ever since he had arrived back in Paris Artaud had been in constant pursuit of drugs. He cadged laudanum wherever he could get it. Prevel's diary contains accounts of many incidents in which Artaud pleaded and begged for relief. He was in great pain. As it later turned out he was suffering from cancer of the anus. When his doctors allowed him as much chloral as he wanted, Artaud realised that he was doomed. One month after the final rejection of his broadcast, on the morning of 4 March 1948 he was found dead, sitting upright at the foot of his bed in his pavilion in the mental hospital of Ivry.

Roger Blin has given an account of how his friends kept vigil, for three days and nights, by his corpse in the little room; not because they believed in such ritual, but to keep away the rats which infested the room by night, and the priests, whom they were afraid Artaud's family might send to give him a religious funeral after all.

To the funeral, without religious rites, at the cemetery of Ivry, the mourners came in two distinct groups: one was formed by Artaud's family, the other by the friends and followers of his last twenty months in Paris.

The feud between the family and the disciples continued for a long time. The family, who had inherited the copyright of Artaud's works, accused the friends of his last period of holding on to drawings and manuscripts which soon became extremely valuable; the disciples reproached the family with heartlessness and greed and a lack of understanding of their son's and brother's work. The publication of Artaud's complete works was delayed for many years by this acrimonious dispute.

Seen in retrospect Artaud's life falls into a pattern and becomes, as he himself so often proclaimed, his supreme work of art. There is an inner logic and consistency in his creation of his youthful image in films like *La Passion de Jeanne d'Arc* to provide a stunning and heart-rending contrast with that of the wizened martyr of society's rejection and contempt which became the image of his final epiphany. And there is a similar deep inner consistency in his gradual abandonment of the conventional objectives of the artist in pursuit of public recognition and fame, the discovery of himself as his supreme subject matter in the correspondence with Rivière, his brief adherence to Surrealism and his final apogee as the poet of utter spontaneity, scattering writings along his way which are no longer craftily-wrought artefacts but bleeding pieces of flesh torn from his living, suffering body. There is even a satisfying meaningfulness in Artaud, the man of the theatre, kept out of the promised land of rebirth and renewal, but, like Moses proclaiming its future laws while glimpsing it from afar, a tragic prophet. But, above all, there is perfection of design in his final descent into madness (if madness it should be called rather than a plumbing of the ultimate depths of human suffering and existential anguish): what else could he have done after the failure of his last theatrical venture, how else could he have even lived through the war and occupation, how else could he, at the end, have emerged as the admired lodestar of a new generation? He had rejected abstract thought and proclaimed the supremacy of concrete experience, and, by the pattern of his living, had incarnated his own conception of art as life and life as suffering.

3   The Limits of Language

'You say you are incapable of expressing your thought. How then do you explain the lucidity and brilliance with which you are expressing the thought that you are incapable of thought?' That, in effect, was the paradox with which Rivière confronted Artaud in their correspondence.

The answer is simple enough: there is a vast difference between a *negative* statement, the bare acknowledgement of the fact that something is *not* there, on the one hand, and the *positive* assertion, on the other, not only that something is present but coupled with an accurate and exhaustive description of its nature, a description capable of fully conveying its quality. That Artaud was able to speak with eloquence about his inability to express his thoughts showed that he possessed the technical qualifications to express thought. Perhaps – and that was implied in Rivière's side of the correspondence – perhaps he had simply nothing, or too little to say. All thought, after all, it could be argued, is verbal, is language; a thought that is incapable of being formulated in words, therefore, by definition would not be a thought, would not exist at all. Artaud had written his poems down; that was what he had had to say and he had said it. If these poems were judged not good enough for publication, how could he claim that the thought he had wanted to express had been better than the expression it had found in his poems?

To what extent can thought exist that is not formulated in words, that stubbornly resists being put into words at all? Are thought and language necessarily co-terminous? Artaud stubbornly persisted in bridging the chasm which seemed to open between his wordless poetic intuitions and their expression in language: 'I am imbecile, through suppression of my thought, by the mal-formation of my thought, I am vacant through the paralysis of my tongue' (*OCI, 116*). Artaud was, at that period of his life, deeply conscious of this possibility. He experienced it as an inner void, a loss of the sense that he existed at all and in a rage of deep frustration.

In an early sketch for a silent film scenario, *Les dix-huit secondes* (18 Seconds), the hero is a young man, an actor,

> who has been struck by a strange disease. He has become incapable of catching his thought; he has retained his entire lucidity; but whatever thought occurs to him, he is incapable of giving it external form, that is to translate it into the appropriate gestures or words. He lacks the words, they no longer respond to his call, he is reduced to seeing images pass inside him, a surfeit of contradictory images, unrelated among themselves. This makes him incapable of mingling with the lives of others or to pursue any activity. (*OCIII, 12*)

It was precisely because Artaud knew that he was suffering from a nervous disease that he persevered in trying to find a solution to the problem, remained convinced that his difficulty in formulating the positive content of his inner world was real and that 'thought' *could* exist in an unformulated, pre-verbal state; and that it should be possible to find ways and means to bridge the gap between this amorphous, as yet uncreated thought, and its expression. Indeed, in the period immediately after the correspondence with Rivière he felt that he had stumbled on a problem of great general importance for the understanding of the process of artistic creation itself. He still saw his condition as a disease, but a disease which, if studied as an extreme particular case of a general condition, could throw light on much more than that one pathological instance. Again and again he attempted to analyse his condition and reached increasing refinement in describing it.

> If it is understood that any idea or image which arises in the unconscious and, through the intervention of the will, is to become a word in the mind, the question then is to find out at what point of its formation the gap opens up, and if, indeed, the manifestation of the will itself is a cause of the trouble, an occasion for that rupture; and whether the rupture occurs at this particular thought or the one which follows. (*OCI Suppl., 140*)

It might even be, he argued in this letter to George Soulié de

Morant, one of the earliest European experts on Chinese acupuncture who was treating him at the time, that it was the very intensity of the as yet unformulated thought, and its rapidity which caused the blockage, manifested externally by his starting to stutter. But then, he continued, it might also be the case that language itself was inadequate to convey what he actually felt:

> If it is cold, I am still able to say that it is cold; but it may also happen that I am incapable of saying it: that is a fact, for there is inside me something wrong from the affective point of view, and if I am asked why I cannot say it, I shall reply that my internal feeling on this fragmentary and insignificant matter simply does not correspond to the three simple little words which I should then have to utter. (*OCI Suppl., 140*)

This assertion had far-reaching implications: perhaps it was not Artaud who was deficient in his inability to express his feelings and turn them into 'thoughts', words, language; perhaps it was language itself which was incapable of expressing them adequately.

During the 1930s, the period when he was evolving his theory of theatre, Artaud became more and more aware of such limitations of language. Having himself experienced the extreme difficulty of finding adequate expression for his ideas and feelings – his thought – he became increasingly contemptuous of writers and other artists using words (such as actors and directors) who seemed to be free of his difficulty. Rightly or wrongly he attributed the ease with which they used language to intellectual laziness and a lack of integrity. Instead of struggling for expression in suffering and torment, as was his lot, they seemed simply to use ready-made formulations which they merely permutated in an endless series of facile re-arrangements. Words, in their hands, had become like a paper currency without backing, conventionalised tokens that had lost all contact with the reality they had once sprung from and were still deemed to represent.

The Surrealist experiment had been one of the ways in which Artaud had tried to renew the potential of language and to break with conventionalised forms of literary expression:

by letting the subconscious itself speak directly and without the intervention of the will, rationality, the awareness of the rules of grammar and rules of elegance of literary form, the Surrealists, and Artaud with them, hoped to widen the potential of language, to make it capable of communicating the actual movement of emotion and the full range of the hidden treasures of human imagination.

Yet Artaud himself did not produce much poetry of significance during his Surrealist period. He was still too preoccupied with his own case, too intent on analysing his disability. It was this disability which led him towards a poetry that did not have to rely on language and could largely do without it – the theatre.

Artaud was not a systematic thinker and never formulated his views on language in a fully developed theory. Yet it is possible to reconstruct the pattern of his thought on the subject.

Basically this amounts to the conviction that it is a profound mistake to equate all human consciousness with that part of it capable of verbal expression. Our consciousness is made up of a multitude of elements only a small part of which is capable of being directly formulated in words. What we see with our eyes, for example, is constantly within our consciousness, yet is very rarely actually put into words or thought about verbally. The same applies to visual memories, or internally visualised wish-fulfilment, day-dreaming. There is the multitude of sounds which surround us or which drift through our imagination. There are the smells impinging upon us, of which we may hardly be conscious because they form a constant background to our lives, but which, at times, are capable of evoking the most powerful associations and memories (one only has to think of Proust's famous *madeleine*). But, above all, there are the numerous body sensations which are constantly felt although they are hardly ever converted into verbal form : the pressure of the clothes we wear upon our skin, the movement of the air in the room and other external influences, as well as those which operate from within us : the rhythm of our heartbeat and our breathing, the tension of our muscles, the fullness or emptiness of our stomachs, etc.

All these are at all times part of our consciousness. And yet when speaking to each other, or, indeed, if we are writers, in formulating our thoughts, we tend to disregard these non-verbal elements of consciousness, although they may well have played an important part in evoking or at least colouring our thought. We tend, on the whole, to equate our consciousness merely with its verbal component, the stream of language that passes through our minds as an unending internal monologue.

It might be thought that we are completely justified in doing so. Aren't these non-verbal elements of consciousness trivial in the extreme?

To a poet, Artaud would argue, it is precisely that non-verbal element of consciousness which is of supreme importance. For it is closely bound up with the very stuff and matter of poetry itself: human emotion.

What is emotion? It may be evoked by words, but it is not, itself, verbal. We are conscious of it, it often overwhelms our consciousness, but emotion certainly belongs to its non-verbal aspect. And if we analyse the nature of emotion, we shall find that it is, however sublimated, however intensified, part and parcel of those very body sensations; that it differs only in degree from such lowly feelings as an over-full stomach or, indeed, Artaud's nagging headaches. For whatever may have set our emotions off, we experience them as body sensations – a quickening of the pulse, a melting relaxation of muscular tensions, a rise in blood-pressure or the release of sex hormones with its various physiological effects. Fear and joy, the sublime beauty of a sunset, the arrival of the beloved or, indeed, the exaltation at hearing a beautiful poem are all ultimately experienced as body sensations.

That is why the three words 'I am cold' seemed to Artaud incapable of conveying what he actually experienced when he felt cold. To communicate emotion, which is the stuff of poetry, abstract words were not enough. That is why poetry makes use of concrete aspects of language which directly communicate to the body, elements such as the musical quality of the words, the sensual nature of the sounds they are made of, the rhythmic quality of the poem which directly activates the body's own rhythms – the beat of the blood, and the vast multitude of non-verbal associations inherent in language and activated by words.

The formula 'I am cold' which abstracts all the body sensation, all the actual and complex feelings connected with one individual's experience of such a physical state, exemplified for Artaud the manner in which too glib a use of language desiccates experience and eventually makes people who rely on such modes of communication and thought lose contact with life itself. They seemed to him to substitute the mathematical formula, the abstract blueprint of experience for the complex fullness of the surging flood of existence in all its richness and complexity.

'The theatre is the only place in the world and the last general means left to us to reach the organism directly, and, in the period of neurosis and low sensuality into which we are about to plunge, to attack that low sensuality by physical means which it will not resist' (*OCIV*, 97). This is how Artaud put his realisation, at which he had arrived by the middle 1930s, that the poetry he wanted to deal in transcended the merely verbal, and that both the instrument to be used in conveying his kind of poetry and the recipient of that poetry, to be exposed to it so as to properly experience its impact, was in fact the human body.

Artaud's ideas about a new technique and practice of theatre (to be discussed in greater detail in the next chapter) are thus basically an attempt to communicate the fullness of human experience and emotion through by-passing the discursive use of language and by establishing contact between the artist and his audience at a level above – or perhaps below – the merely cerebral appeal of the verbal plane. As, at that stage, he felt, or perhaps indeed *was*, incapable of bringing to bear the infinite variety of powerful and subtle techniques by which poetry *can* in fact be made capable of having so profound an impact that the fullness of human emotion, spiritual as well as physical, is communicated, he was burning to find ways and means of transmitting his experience, his physical suffering, his physical exaltation directly to the minds and bodies of other human beings. And to achieve that, he felt, he had to 'smash language in order to touch life' (*OCIV*, 18).

This is how we have to understand his use of the term 'a theatre of cruelty': he wanted the theatre to swoop down among a crowd of spectators with all the awesome horror of the plague, the Black Death of the Middle Ages, with all its shattering impact, creating a complete upheaval, physical, mental and moral, among the populations it struck.

'The theatre like the plague' he proclaims in perhaps the most powerfully poetic of the essays in *The Theatre and its Double*, '*Le Théâtre et la Peste*',

> is a crisis which is resolved either in death or in the return to complete health. The plague is a superior evil because it is a total crisis after which nothing is left except death or utter purification. So also the theatre is an evil because it is the supreme state of balance which cannot be reached without destruction. It asks the spirit to partake in a delirium which vastly enhances its energies . . .
> (*OCIV*, 38-9)

Statements like these display the fanatical fury with which Artaud pursued his objective, a commitment of truly mad heroism. The new language of the theatre, a superior instrument of communication beyond the mere discursive use of concepts, language and words, would establish a link through which the totality of emotion could freely flow from body to body, from actor to spectator. And this, in breaking down the barriers between human beings, in enabling them to partake in each other's most shattering emotions, would achieve no less than a new communion of mankind, a total transformation of society and through it give to all human existence a greater richness and higher quality.

It is a grandiose vision, powered – one can feel this in the prophetic sweep of the essays in *The Theatre and its Double* – by the very rage and fury of frustration accumulated through his desperate efforts to bridge the gap between his feeling and its verbal expression. It is as though Artaud wanted to unleash the pent-up energies of this frustration in a vast liberating outburst of violence, of aggression against an unfeeling outside world, visualised as a mass of complacent, apathetic spectators in the theatre who would find themselves engulfed, overwhelmed and compelled to feel, to suffer as deeply as he himself, Antonin Artaud, had suffered.

If language alone had proved incapable of communicating the actual physical sensation of his painful struggles to other people, perhaps an assault upon their senses in the theatre might wake them from their indifference and, by plunging them into equivalent pain and anguish, open their minds, shake them out of their apathy and thus purify them morally. Artaud himself, always extremely lucid about his mental state, was fully aware of this rage, the pent-up aggression behind all his efforts. 'Do you know another man', he wrote to Breton in 1937, shortly before his departure to Ireland, 'whose indignation against everything which exists at present is as steady and violent; and who is so constantly and violently in a state of perpetual fulmination? This rage which consumes me, and of which every day I learn to make better use, must have some meaning' (*OCIV*, 38-9).

Even more than against the complacent bourgeois who neither knew nor cared for his suffering, this rage was directed against the system of thought, the whole cultural climate which had produced that attitude. Was not the complacency of these people built on the ideal of reason, moderation, *bienséance* which had animated French society for so long? And was not that ideal, in turn, the outcome of a belief in logic and thus ultimately in the correct use of language and reason as instruments of self-control. It was through an excessive reliance on the ability of logical discourse to find a just – and always moderate – solution to all problems that the springs of true feeling had been drained. Having left France for a country he believed nearer to these sources and still nourished by uncorrupted emotion, Mexico, Artaud warned his Mexican friends against the rationalism of Europe and the temptation to Mexicans to find themselves the heirs of 'the Latin spirit, rational culture, the supremacy of reason' (*OCVIII*, 266). They still had, so Artaud believed, access to a richer experience through ritual, magic, and surrender to the wild transports of peyotl.

And yet the hopes that Artaud had pinned on the theatre and his own ability to create a new language of physically embodied poetry came to nought. It is a tragic irony that it was through this collapse of his expectations and the breakdown it caused that he eventually bridged the chasm that had yawned between his emotion and its transmutation into words, and that he found his very own poetic language, a mode of utterance so powerful and direct that it was indeed capable of fully conveying the poet's emotion right down to the physical level of body sensations.

In writing to Soulié de Morant Artaud had wondered whether it was the intervention of the *will*, the conscious desire and determination to express himself, which made the thought and the emotion, wanting to be expressed, evaporate. In the mental turmoil which followed the catastrophe of *The Cenci* and the deep disappointment after his return from Mexico Artaud reached such a pitch of nervous excitement that this last barrier of self-consciousness finally gave way. The *will*, the element of critical self-awareness which, in searching for the best possible turn of phrase, the most elegant image, had blocked the free flow between emotion and utterance, was swept aside in the wild exaltation of an artist who had, he felt, become an instrument of higher powers, a magician, a miracle-working prophet. The breathless frenzy with which he proclaimed his mission to save the world from impending doom imbues a text like that of *Les Nouvelles Révelations de l'Etre*, never intended to be poetry, with a sweep and intensity of vision that transmutes its language into that of a sublime poem. A poem, moreover, which, in its impact, its power to stir the imagination and the senses, is far superior to anything Artaud himself ever was able to achieve in the theatre.

This inspired breakthrough into poetry was followed by years of stunned, catatonic silence in the asylums of Sotteville-lès-Rouen, Sainte-Anne and Ville-Evrard. But after Artaud's arrival at Rodez, and even more so in the last frantic twenty months after his return to Paris, that seething, flaming lava-stream of language flowed again. Writing feverishly by day and by night Artaud produced an unceasing output of direct utterance in the form of essays, letters, personal confessions, rhythmic prose, glossolalia and inarticulated combinations of consonants. It is difficult to decide which of these writings should be classified as poems, for all are deeply poetic, simply because they are direct and unalloyed expressions of profound emotion and triumphantly succeed in communicating that emotion through language.

It is another strange irony that in this phase of his career, many years after being expelled from the Surrealist movement, Artaud should have realised the original aims of that movement more truly and more totally than any of the poets the Surrealists had themselves produced: for not even the greatest among these, whether Eluard, Desnos or Aragon, had ever fully renounced the use of their technique, the intervention of their shaping critical intelligence in putting their poems on paper. Artaud in his prophetic fury – or madness as it seemed to many – really allowed his wounded spirit to flow freely and without restraint; he fully attained the Surrealists' objective, their search for a technique of automatic writing which would give access to the darkest, deepest layers of the human mind and capture its movement at the very moment it emerged from the chasms and abysses of the unconscious into the light of consciousness, as poetry. Artaud himself, twenty-five years earlier, had been the director of the research centre set up by the Surrealists to investigate ways and means by which this objective could be achieved. Now he had become a living example of its attainment; but he had found the solution not, as he had then thought, by producing a neatly-argued paper in smooth theoretical terms, but by having become himself the incarnation of that solution – that this type of poetry could only be achieved through a terrifying descent – or perhaps an ascent – to hitherto unplumbed regions of human suffering and total self-abandonment. Abandoning all restraint, all intention of pleasing, of giving shape or formal perfection to his utterance and letting his wild fantasies, his fury and anguish, his pain and torment roar out, Artaud succeeded in evoking that very physical impact, that gut-reaction which had been the objective of his theatrical endeavours. He wanted to make his last public appearance, the abortive radio programme *Pour en finir avec le jugement de Dieu*, the true fulfilment of his ideas about the theatre of cruelty: yet this was simply a sequence of texts orchestrated for four voices and some percussion instruments. The performance, in particular Artaud's own spine-chilling screams and banging of gongs, added something to its impact, but its true 'cruelty' (in the Artaudian sense of physical evocation of emotion) resides very largely in the words themselves, whether technically these texts should be regarded as polemical pamphlets, autobiographical meditations or 'poems'. Such is the degree of obsessiveness, of Artaud's possession by the passions which convulse him, that they appear as madly inspired as the utterances of the Pythia at Delphoi talking in a holy trance, or the chants of a shaman through whom the voices of Gods and Demons speak.

It is difficult to analyse the means by which Artaud's writings at this period make their impact. *What* they say (and what might be described as the discursive or conceptual element) is so wildly outside the customary bounds of reason that it contributes as much to their physical impact (through the sheer amazement or terror such descriptions inspire) as the way *how* they say it, the furious discordance and variation of the rhythms, the abrupt transitions, the intensity evoked by repetition and accumulation of words, all combining to communicate the rage, anguish and deep commitment which underlie them. Here language truly reaches its uttermost limit.

4 The Artaudian Theatre —
Theory and Practice

> The theatre
> > is the state
> > the place
> > the point
>
> where we can get hold of man's anatomy and
> through it heal and dominate life. . . .
> > Artaud (from *Aliéner l'Acteur*, 12 May 1947)

Artaud's ideas about the theatre changed and developed a great deal throughout his life. But from the very beginning of his active involvement he was a fanatical believer in its mission, its power to change Society, Man and the World, its revolutionary potential and redemptive force. He despised the view that the theatre was a mere place of entertainment. 'There are those who go to the theatre as they go to the brothel' he started an article for a Marseilles paper while working with Dullin, '. . . One might say that at this moment there are two different types of theatre: a spurious theatre, facile and false, the theatre frequented by bourgeois, military men, rentiers, shopkeepers, winemerchants, teachers of water-colour painting, adventurers, whores and winners of the *Prix de Rome*, which takes place at Sacha Guitry's, on the Boulevards and in the Comédie Française; and another theatre which finds a roof over its head where it can, but which is a theatre conceived as the achievement of mankind's purest aspirations' (*OCII, 175*).

In this attitude he belonged to the mainstream of the movement for a renovation of the theatre which had started as a reaction to its mid-nineteenth century degradation into cheap melodrama and vulgar entertainment and was led by men like Ibsen, Strindberg and Shaw, the Duke of Meiningen, Nietzsche, Richard Wagner, Adolphe Appia, Gordon Craig, Max Reinhardt and Stanislavsky; and in France Antoine, Lugné-Poe, Copeau, Gémier. Dullin, Pitoeff and Jouvet with

whom Artaud was, in one way or another, connected in his
professional career as an actor and director were the immediate heirs of this tradition, just as Jean-Louis Barrault and
Roger Blin, who worked with Artaud in their beginnings,
can be seen as its champions who continued it to our own
days. Yet, while Artaud clearly forms part of this theatrical
mainstream, he was also deeply at odds with it. For all its
earnestness and reforming zeal, this movement for a return
to theatre as a serious art form had always remained within
the framework of society; its standard-bearers and practition-
ers had worked within its professional and financial possibilities. Artaud's belief in the redemptive power of the
theatre, on the other hand, was so radical and uncompromising that he was in perpetual conflict with the established forms
of theatrical enterprise. Yet to earn a living, and to gain a
chance of working at all, he had, somehow, to come to terms
with the world of theatre owners, impresarios, influential
patrons and potential financial backers, and the tensions these
attempts created within him proved well-nigh unbearable. In
trying to understand Artaud's writings on the theatre, therefore, one must always remember that his mind was frequently working at two distinct levels : in drawing up mani-
festos for his various projects he was, at one and the same
time, enunciating his sweeping revolutionary ideas and trying
to re-assure the influential people he needed to support him.
Thus, in the *First Manifesto of the Theatre of Cruelty* in
October 1932, which proclaimed his determination to diminish
the importance of the playwright as against the director, he
included the project of a production of Buechner's *Woyzeck*,
of which his patron Jean Paulhan, editor of the *NRF* was
co-translator 'in a spirit of reaction against our principles
and as an example of what one can achieve on the stage
with a precise text' (*OCIV, 119*). By far the most glaring, and
disastrous, example of the tension between Artaud's theoretical
ideas and his need to try and find a *modus vivendi* with the
theatre as it was at that time is the production of *The Cenci*
in which he had to cast an inexperienced actress because she
gave him access to funds, use a theatre building totally at
variance with his ideas and, in the final analysis, produce
a play which, although he himself had written it, was far
removed from his ideal of a theatre beyond a conventional
text, and the traditional structure of classical tragedy, based

on the movement of large numbers of performers in an open space.

It might be argued that had his ideas been less extreme he might have found it easier to gain a foothold in the theatrical establishment: or conversely that, had he found a foothold in the theatrical establishment sooner, say as a result of his work with the Théâtre Alfred Jarry, his ideas might never have become so extreme. It is difficult, however, to believe that the latter could ever have been the case. The programmatic statements for the Théâtre Alfred Jarry already contain the essence of Artaud's most radical concepts; the very first announcement of that enterprise already makes the demand that the theatre should never be mere play: 'If the theatre is not just play, if it is a true reality, by what means can we give it that degree of reality, make each performance a kind of event [*une sorte d'évènement* could also be translated as 'a kind of *happening*' – surely the first use of that term in this context!], that is the problem we have to solve' (*OCII*, 19). It is this first manifesto (published in the *NRF* for November 1926) which describes a police raid on a brothel as the ideal theatrical event (or happening) and insists that each member of the audience, on leaving the theatre,

should have been shaken and taken aback by the internal power of the performance and that that power should be in direct relation to the anxieties and preoccupations of his life. The illusion will no longer be dependent on the probability or improbability of the action, but on the power to communicate and the reality of that action . . . It is not to the mind or senses of the audience that we address ourselves but to their entire existence. Theirs and ours . . . (*OCII*, 21)

The concept of the Theatre of Cruelty is already present in these fighting words. And at about the same time Artaud (as the spokesman of his associates in the venture of the Théâtre Alfred Jarry) leaves no doubt about the sweep of his, and their, ambitions:

we are aiming at no less than to go back to the human or inhuman sources of the theatre and to revive it totally. Everything which forms part of the opacity and magnetic fascination of dreams, all this, these dark layers of consciousness . . . we want to see it triumph on the stage, at the risk of losing ourselves and exposing ourselves to the ridicule of a terrible failure . . . We see the theatre as a *truly magical* enterprise. We address ourselves not to the eyes, not to the direct emotion of the mind; what we are trying to create is a certain *psychological* emotion in which the most secret recesses of the heart will be brought into the open. (*OCII, 30-1*)

Here are the guiding ideas of *The Theatre and its Double*, if not yet fully formed and elaborated, at least already clearly recognisable: the theatre as reality; the demand for an impact on the audience which amounts to an imposition of suffering on them, i.e. cruelty; the demand that the theatre should be able to communicate deep, subconscious and therefore not yet verbalised emotion directly to the spectator by means that amount to nothing less than magic. Yet it was not until after the overwhelming experience of encountering the Balinese dancers in 1931 that Artaud's attitude to theatre finally crystallised and acquired its explosive power which can still be felt today. What was it that gave *The Theatre and its Double* that force?

In his book, *Antonin Artaud et l'Essence du Théâtre*, M. Henri Gouhier of the Institut de France questions Artaud's frequent demand that the theatre should return to its origins in religious ritual; he points out that while there is much great art which is religious, much very bad art, like those sugary statues in Catholic churches, is able to invoke genuine religious feeling; while there is also much very great art which is utterly non-religious. Art, therefore, he argues, quite correctly, can only be great art if it fulfills *artistic* criteria which are independent of religious considerations; and, indeed, if the theatre's origins are in religious ritual, it became an art form precisely at the moment when the theatre separated from ritual and turned into an autonomous activity. All this is convincing enough but it misses Artaud's point: for Artaud the theatre was not just a religious art, an art form serving a religion; for him the theatre was a manifestation of the religious impulse itself. *His religion was the theatre* – at least up to the point when his profoundly religious nature led him into other, even more intense and impassioned manifestations of his yearning to transcend the world as he had found it.

Yet how can the theatre, a technique of communication which is generally regarded as capable of expressing a multitude of contents and messages and is therefore necessarily neutral, free of its own philosophy or ideology, be turned into a religion? What kind of religion could the theatre be?

For Artaud the theatre was 'activated metaphysics' (*OCIV*, 54). 'The reservoir of energies which is constituted by Myths no longer incarnated by mankind, the theatre incarnates them' (*OCV*, 272). The theatre is the double (that is to say, the representative) 'of that great magic active force (*agent*) of which the theatre through its form is the figuration until the time when it becomes its transfiguration' (*OCV*, 272-3). And what are these great magic powers with which the theatre can re-establish connection? They are 'the secret truths' which the theatre can again bring to light through its language of gesture, 'that part of the truth buried under the forms in their encounter with the flow of Becoming' (*OCV*, 84). For all its seeming vagueness, the message is clear enough: like Bergson, Shaw or Nietzsche Artaud was a Romantic vitalist, a believer in the healing power of the life force, the power of man's natural instinct as against dry-as-dust rationalism, logical reasoning based on linguistic subtlety; he supported the heart against the head, the body and its emotions against the rarefied abstractions of the mind. And if Nietzsche in *The Birth of Tragedy* had proclaimed his conviction that the basis of the theatre is the spirit of Dionysos, dark, violent, turbulent, passionate, inarticulate in its musical ecstasy, but tempered and tamed by Apollonian clarity, measure and reason, Artaud rejected the Apollonian element altogether and put his trust in the dark forces of Dionysian vitality with all their violence and mystery. If these forces could be activated through the theatre, incarnated by the theatre, Artaud hoped that mankind might be diverted from their disastrous path that led towards an increasing atrophying of their instincts which amounted to the death of their vitality and eventual extinction.

Artaud's position also has parallels with Freud's view that the malaise in Western civilisation was due to the repression of so much of man's instinctive, subconscious, impulsive life. A great deal of Surrealist ideology was based on Freudian concepts and Artaud was clearly influenced by Freud, in particular the *Interpretation of Dreams*. It was Freud who had indicated how language in dream is transposed into images which can then be read like picture-writing, hieroglyphs. Hence Artaud, in his endeavour to reactivate the subconscious and to appeal to it directly, preached a return to communication at this level. 'It is not a question of suppressing articulate speech, but to give it something of the importance it has in dreams' (*OCIV*, *112*). But, above all, if the Dionysiac stands for the instinct and the body and the Apollonian for the abstraction of bloodless reason and the mind, the theatre is the means through which the body can again be given its due importance. Artaud's idea of a metaphysical theatre, paradoxically, springs from his conviction that it is abstract, discursive thinking which cuts man off from the hidden, mysterious sources of his being and confines him in a narrow mundane world. To re-establish contact with the true meta-physical basis of human existence it is the body which must be re-awakened and re-activated: in other words to reach the metaphysical sphere we have to become more physical. It was the revelation of the mysterious forces which rule the universe through their strange movements and hieratic costumes, the miraculous music that accompanied their dance, the presence of cosmic power in their inarticulate cries, which made Artaud's discovery of the Balinese dancers such a decisive event in his life and made him realise the true nature of the theatre as a potential instrument for the redemption of mankind. 'I am not one of those who believe that civilisation should change so that the theatre can change; but I believe that the theatre used in a higher, and the most difficult possible, sense has the power to influence the nature and development of things' (*OCIV*, *95*).

In the theatre, in Artaud's view, the cosmic forces, made manifest through physical means, can reach and touch the submerged physical, non-verbal and subconscious energies of the masses, hence his concept of a theatre of cruelty:

> But 'theatre of cruelty' means, above all, a theatre difficult and cruel for myself. And on the level of performance it is not a matter of the cruelty we bring to bear upon each other in mutually cutting up our bodies, sawing at our

personal anatomies or, like Assyrian Emperors,[1] sending ourselves through the post bags of human ears, noses or
nostrils nicely cut up, but of that much more terrible and
necessary cruelty which things can exercise upon ourselves.
We are not free. The heavens can still fall upon our heads.
And the theatre exists, in the first place, to teach us that.
(*OCIV*, 95)

Yet, even though sublimated into forms subtler than direct
physical assault, the Artaudian theatre still relies on physical
or near-physical action:

If music has an effect on snakes, this is not due to the
spiritual concepts that it transmits to them, but because
snakes are elongated and lie in long coils on the ground,
which their body touches over almost their total length;
and the musical vibrations which are propagated in the
soil reach it as a very long and subtle massage; well, I
intend to do to the audience what snake-charmers do and
to make them reach even the subtlest notions through
their organism . . . (*OCIV*, 97-8)

Artaud regarded the theatre's ability (as he postulated it)
to act physically upon a crowd of spectators without actually
hurting their bodies as its chief distinguishing mark, and,
curiously, one that it shared with the plague. In his essay
on 'The Theatre and the Plague' he dwells at length on the
fact that, although filled with a black liquid, the body of the
victim who has died of the plague, shows no organic lesions.
This, he argues, is comparable to

the state of the actor whom his emotions totally over-
whelm and shatter without an effect on reality. Everything in the physical aspect of the actor, as in that of the
plague victim, shows that life has reacted to a paroxysm,
and yet nothing has happened . . . Where the images of
the plague in relation with a powerful state of physical
disorganisation are like the last explosions of a spiritual
force that is exhausting itself, the poetic images of the
theatre are a spiritual force which starts its trajectory
in the senses and can then transcend reality. Once launched
into his fury the actor needs infinitely more virtue to stop
himself from committing a crime than an assassin needs

courage to commit his; and it is here that the action of an emotion in the theatre, in its purity (*gratuité* i.e. disinterestedness appears as infinitely more valid that that of an emotion carried to the point of realisation in action. (*OCIV, 30-1*)

In other words, the emotions in their manifestation in body sensations are *real* and true in a physical sense both in the actor and ultimately in the audience, but the actions which these emotions would in the real world entail remain potential: 'a real theatrical experience shakes the calm of the senses, liberates the compressed unconscious and drives towards a kind of potential revolt, which, however, cannot realise its full value, unless it remains potential and imposes on the assembled crowd a difficult and heroic attitude' (*OCIV, 34*).

The theatre, as seen by Artaud in *The Theatre and its Double*, is essentially a religious ritual the content, the underlying myth of which is the theatre itself; that is, the theatre defined as an assembly of human beings striving to establish contact with the profound mainsprings of their own being, the dark forces of physical emotion which lie beyond the trivialities of their everyday existence. The theatre enables them to experience the full reality of these emotions without involving them in irreversible real life situations in which alone experiences of such shattering power could otherwise be lived through. And by making the full force of a full emotional life, the whole gamut of human suffering and joy again active in multitudes of human beings, the theatre could change their basic attitude to life and institutions, their ways of thinking, their entire consciousness and thus transform society and the world.

But *how*, by what means and methods is all this to be accomplished?

Above all, the playwright disappears as the main fountainhead of the theatrical experience. This, for Artaud, was the principal and overwhelming lesson of the Balinese theatre: 'The Balinese realise, with the utmost rigour, the idea of a pure theatre, in which everything, conception as well as execution is valid and exists only in the measure in which it is objectivised *on the stage*. They victoriously demonstrate the absolute preponderance of the director whose creative

power *eliminates the words*' (*OCIV*, 64-5). Artaud's theatre is
essentially a director's theatre with the director acting as a
poet using the concrete language of the whole gamut of
physical existence from abstract space to the minutest nuance
of the actor's bodily movement.

This stage language will not dispense with words, but
will use them as they appear in dreams and will draw the
fullest possible effect from the quality of words as objects
with a physical existence, as sounds in cries, sobs, incantation and an infinite variety of expressive colours. A technique will have to be found for recording and transcribing
the multitude of modes of expression of the non-verbal
language of the stage; for each gesture, each movement, each
intonation will have a definite and precise expressive meaning
comparable to that of Chinese ideograms or Egyptian hiero-
glyphics. Yet, unlike those systems of signs which have to
be laboriously learned, the new stage language of concrete
signs will have the power of immediately communicating the
exact meaning of each hieroglyphic sign or symbol to the
audience. This communicative power which springs from
the direct physical impact achieved by what happens on
the stage constitutes the true magic of the theatre.

The largest theatrical element with a direct and immediate
physical impact is the space in which the theatrical event
occurs. The traditional theatre building will be abandoned.
In the Artaudian theatre there will be no barrier between
actors and audience. 'The spectator placed in the middle of
the action is enveloped and covered by it' (*OCIV*, 115). At
first hangars or barns already in existence can be used for
this purpose, later special buildings will be constructed on
the pattern of certain churches or 'certain temples in the
highlands of Tibet' (*OCIV*, 115). The audience will be seated
in the middle of these spaces on seats which will be moveable
so that they can follow the action developing around them on
all sides. The walls of the auditorium will be whitewashed in
light-absorbing chalk. An elevated gallery running right round
the auditorium will enable the action to take place at several
levels. There will be no *scenery*. The splendour of the *costumes* will be sufficient to give the action vividness and
colour, particularly as each costume will convey its own
precise hieroglyphic meaning. Modern dress with its drab-
ness and suggestion of the naturalistic and psychologising

conventional theatre should be avoided. On the other hand wholly new and revolutionary *lighting* equipment will have to be designed to produce magical effects of great impact and meaning; these will have to include vibrating light, waves of light or veritable explosions of light resembling fireworks. The light will have to have a wide variety of colour and tonal qualities such as tenseness, density and opacity to produce the impression of warmth, cold, fury or fear. *Music* and *sound* will also have to play a very important part; ancient and forgotten instruments may have to be used, or completely new ones invented, some of which will have to be able to produce 'sounds which cannot be endured' (*OCIV*, 114). And of course natural sounds, which Artaud used with stereophonic effect in his production of *The Cenci*, also enter into the arsenal of auditory effects which will form part of the new stage language. Artaud attached special importance also to large puppets which would appear in the action and produce magical effects of dreamlike fantasy or surprise. In the *First Manifesto of the Theatre of Cruelty* he makes an enigmatic reference to 'puppets thirty feet high, representing King Lear's beard in the storm' (*OCIV*, 117).

Although always ritual and magic, the Artaudian theatre is by no means to be without humour. Indeed the element of humour, which Artaud conceived as a dislocation of sensibility through anarchy, the juxtaposition of incompatible elements which turns the expected order of things upside down, is to play an important part in the peculiar poetic ambiance of his theatrical creations. He quotes, as an example, a scene from a Marx Brothers film (he loved the Marx Brothers and included a note on them in *The Theatre and its Double*) in which a man who thinks he is about to kiss a beautiful lady suddenly finds that he is holding a cow in his arms. Artaud was fully aware that his conception of a theatre in the round with full audience involvement approached old traditions of spectacle hitherto on the margin of theatre like the Circus and the Music Hall, Burlesque and Vaudeville. He wanted to draw every possible lesson from these.

What then, finally, in this director's theatre, about the actor? His role, said Artaud in a letter to Gaston Gallimard at the time he was planning to launch a theatre with the support of the *NRF*, is 'at the same time extremely important and extremely limited. What one calls the personality of the

actor must disappear completely. There can no longer be
an actor who imposes his rhythm on the *ensemble* and to
whose personality everything must be subordinated . . . In
the theatre the actor as such must no longer have the right
to any initiative whatever' (*OCV, 125*). On the other hand,
as a theatre based on a complex language of fixed signs, ges-
tures and expressions will require very great skill, the Artaudian theatre will need 'strong' actors 'who will be chosen not
because of their talent but on the strength of a kind of vital
sincerity, which is stronger than their convictions' (*OCV, 126*).
Already in the prospectus of the Théâtre Alfred Jarry Artaud
had promised that the performances directed by him 'would
proceed in the manner of a perforated music roll in a mechanical piano . . . and would give to the auditorium the impression of fatality and the most precise predetermination'
(*OCII, 61-2*).[2]

On the other hand Artaud devoted much thought to the
techniques of acting. One of the most remarkable of the
essays in *The Theatre and its Double*, which, though least
often quoted and understood, has had the most far-reaching
influence in that it helped Jean-Louis Barrault to develop his
theory of acting, is '*Un Athlétisme Affectif*' (which might be
rendered as 'The Actor, an Athlete of his Emotions'). In it,
based on the teaching of the Cabbala, Artaud develops a
system of triads of breathing and expressive techniques which
allow him to lay the foundation for a complete and complex
system in which each type of breath corresponds to a basic
emotional colour which can then be infinitely varied by per-
mutation and combination. Artaud's language is obscure and
it is, above all, difficult to visualise what he means without
direct demonstration by a teacher. But the basis is a number
of triads based on, for example, (1) breathing in (2) breathing
out and (3) retaining the breath. Linking one's mode of utterance to each of these three possibilities produces distinct
expressive colours; so does another triad, such as placing
the voice (1) in the diaphragm, (2) in the chest, or (3) in
the head. Taking these six expressive possibilities as the
primary colours one can then vary and permutate them by
placing the voice in the head while breathing out, or in, or
retaining the breath and so on. Artaud uses concepts like
masculine, feminine and neuter and makes reference to *yin*
and *yang* and the 380 points of Chinese acupuncture. If one

knows how to translate this technical and mystical language into mundane physical practice the results, as anyone who has watched Barrault demonstrate this technique (or rather his elaboration of it) can testify, are spectacular. As Artaud says in his essay, it is through breathing and other physical links that the identification between the actor's and the spectator's body is established. This is the chain which links them together and 'allows the spectator to identify himself with the performance breath by breath, and bar by bar . . . All emotion has organic bases. It is in cultivating his emotion in his body that the actor recharges the density of its voltage. Knowing in advance which parts of the body one wants to touch means putting the spectator into magic trances' (*OCIV*, 163).

So much for the actor in the Artaudian theatre. And who should form its public? In the *First Manifesto of the Theatre of Cruelty* Artaud deals with the matter thus: 'The Public: First the theatre must exist' (*OCIV, 118*).

This, in brief outline, is Artaud's view of a new theatre, as described in the essays collected in *The Theatre and its Double*, written between 1931 and 1936. *The First Manifesto of the Theatre of Cruelty* (published in October 1932) contained an impressive list of projected performances: an adaptation of an English Elizabethan play, perhaps *Arden of Faversham* which André Gide was translating; a poetic drama by Léon-Paul Fargue; an adaptation of a story from the *Zohar*, Rabbi Siméon; the story of Blue-Beard, as reconstructed from the archives; the Fall of Jerusalem, according to the Bible and history; an adaptation of a story by the Marquis de Sade; one of several romantic melodramas the very improbability of which would become a poetic element; Buechner's *Woyzeck*; and some works of the Elizabethan theatre, stripped of their text so that only characters, plot and period flavour remain. In the *Second Manifesto of the Theatre of Cruelty*, issued as a prospectus in 1933, only one performance is projected, Artaud's own *Conquest of Mexico* which existed as a scenario, a blueprint for a production to be created in rehearsal. When all these plans finally materialised in 1935 with *The Cenci*, relatively little of Artaud's theoretical concepts could be translated into practice. There was the music emanating from loudspeakers in the four corners of the auditorium and there was Artaud's own frantic acting, but the sets and costumes, though excellent, were conventional and so was the play.

To judge by the consensus of the opinion of those who saw Artaud act in the theatre he was certainly an uneven, probably rather a bad actor. Barrault is on record that

> he took drugs which tranquillised him or pepped him up or gave him the illusion that he had found a certain equilibrium; he was rather like a man in a dream who thinks he has solved a problem while dreaming and then, on the next morning, when he wakes up his problem has remained unsolved. There were certainly sublime moments in his acting, but they were suddenly contradicted by dissonances over which he had no control.[3]

As a director, in the case of *The Cenci*, he had difficulty in explaining to the actors what he wanted them to do. Blin has described how, in arranging the banquet scene in *The Cenci* Artaud told the actors who were playing the guests to assume, each of them, the movements of a different animal and that the actors simply did not know how to put that suggestion into practice. Whether with sufficient means and time at his disposal Artaud could ever have succeeded in putting his own ideas into practice must remain an open question.

During his period of confinement Artaud only occasionally revived his interest in the theatre. His religious instinct had found other, and even more passionately committed outlets. But after his return from Rodez he again talked about the theatre and wrote poems about it. But in most of these the term theatre itself appears in a different sense: it seems almost as though the terms 'theatre' and 'life' had become interchangeable:

> The true theatre has always seemed to me as the exercise
> of a terrible and dangerous act
> in which, moreover, the idea of theatre and performance is
> eliminated just as
> that of all science, all religion and all art . . .[4]

Or even:

And now I want to say something which might perhaps
astonish many people.
I am the enemy
of the theatre.
I have always been that.
As much as I love the theatre,
As much am I, for that very reason, its enemy . . .[5]

In many of these deeply-moving poems the spectre of the
theatre seems to float across Artaud's consciousness, with
many of the metaphysical ideas and the religious fervour of
his belief in its redemptive mission still shining through,
almost like memories only half recalled :

The plague,
cholera,
the black pocks only
exist because the dance
and consequently the theatre
have not yet begun to exist . . .[6]

When the radio programme *Pour en finir avec le jugement de
Dieu* was in preparation it was said that Artaud regarded
this as the first real public presentation of his ideas of a
Theatre of Cruelty, just as to some observers his courageous
and heart-rending exposure of his sufferings at the public
lecture at the Vieux Colombier in January 1947 had seemed
the ultimate merging of reality and its public exhibition
as a performance – hence the true theatre of cruelty. After
the banning of the broadcast Artaud wrote to his friend
Paule Thévenin who had helped him so much in its creation
and announced, deeply disappointed, that he had for ever
given up the idea of working through a mechanical medium :

Where the machine is
there is always an abyss and nothingness . . .

And he went on :

. . . .
And I shall henceforth devote myself
exclusively

    to the theatre
    as I understand it
    a theatre of blood
    a theatre which at every performance will have achieved
        some gain

    bodily
    to him who plays as well as to him who comes to see
        the playing,

    moreover
    one doesn't play
    one acts.
    The theatre is in reality the *genesis* of creation.
    It will be done.

This poem in the form of a letter is dated 24 February 1948. Artaud died on 4 March.

It is impossible to read *The Theatre and its Double* or an account of its contents today without realising how powerful and widespread its influence has proved to be. It took a long time for that influence to make itself felt, particularly in France. Barrault and Blin, the two major younger directors who had been under Artaud's most immediate influence in their formative years, both went their own ways. Barrault has said that he derived great benefit from Artaud's method of the expressive triads, but he also remained firmly wedded for many years to a theatre based on accepted texts; he even became the chief proponent of Artaud's early *bête noire*, Claudel. Roger Blin, whose work served writers who had been close personal friends of Artaud, like Arthur Adamov, as well as playing a part in bringing to prominence such giants of the post-war avantgarde as Beckett and Genet, has himself pointed out that Artaud's influence on him was, in the main, an indirect one in that it showed him a model of total dedication and uncompromising artistic purity, rather than leading him to adopt any specifically Artaudian style or method.

Outside France Artaud's influence on the theatre came into its own after the rise to fame and prominence of the post-war French avantgarde had drawn the attention of those interested in the art of drama to the tradition that stretches from Jarry, Apollinaire and the Surrealists to Beckett and Ionesco.

The part Artaud had played in shaping that tradition was gradually being recognised after a translation of *The Theatre and its Double* had appeared in the United States in 1958.

Peter Brook and Charles Marowitz gave public recognition to the discovery of Artaud as one of the founders of modern avantgarde theatre by calling their 1964 season of experimental acting and staging at the LAMDA theatre (which was to prepare the Royal Shakespeare Company's ensemble for the difficult task of producing Genet's *The Screens* under Peter Brook's direction; a project which never reached fruition in public) 'Theatre of Cruelty'. This highly successful evening, which essentially amounted to a training session or rehearsal in public, included what must have been the first performance of Artaud's sketch *Le Jet de Sang* (The Spurt of Blood), a skit on a romantically-lyrical piece by Salacrou, dating from 1925. While this early playlet did not demonstrate Artaud's ideas very clearly, other experiments inspired by his demand for expression without the use of articulate language and a heightened expressiveness of the body proved highly interesting. The ten actors who had been trained by Brook and Marowitz during this experimental season – they included Glenda Jackson – became the nucleus of Brook's highly successful production of Peter Weiss's *Marat/Sade* by the RSC which again made use of Artaud's ideas, particularly in the treatment of madness in the portrayal of the majority of the characters who are inmates of a lunatic asylum. Peter Brook's further researches at his experimental workshop in Paris in later years also centred on Artaud's postulate of a theatre transcending the limitations of language. Brook tried to evolve an expressive idiom based on gesture, movement and incantatory sound, which would be understood even without a knowledge of the meaning of the words which might be involved. These efforts culminated in a spectacle, created for the Festival at Persepolis in 1971, for which Brook asked the poet Ted Hughes to invent a wholly new language 'Orghast' designed to be expressive through sound alone. Peter Brook's more conventional work, notably his widely acclaimed *A Midsummer Night's Dream*, applied some of the lessons learned from these experiments with brilliant success: here too Artaud's influence could be seen in the emphasis on physical expressiveness and acrobatic prowess in the acting, the techniques of the circus and music hall used in the staging and the way in which truly *magical* effects were produced by a combination of subtle refinement and artless naivety, very much in the spirit of the Balinese – and other Oriental folk traditions – so highly praised and recommended by Artaud.

Jerzy Grotowski, the brilliant Polish director, whose ideas and practice have very much in common with Artaud, had no knowledge of Artaud's writings until after he had achieved international fame and success. Nevertheless the similarity between Artaud and Grotowski is striking. This is probably due to the fact that Grotowski, who wanted to study theatre outside his native Poland, was sent by the Polish authorities to another Eastern country, China; hence he received much of his inspiration from theatrical techniques very near to the Oriental models Artaud admired. Grotowski, like Artaud, believes in the theatre as a metaphysical force, only justified if it can truly transform the lives of both actors and spectators. He demands a dedication from his company which amounts, just as Artaud postulated, to a veritable immersion in the theatre as a holy rite and quasi-religious practice. Like Artaud Grotowski uses incantation and extracts maximum expressiveness from the human body. He insists on audiences of no more than about forty or fifty spectators, in order to expose them to the most direct physical impact from the actors. Like Artaud, Grotowski insists on the abandonment of the conventional theatre architecture; he creates a wholly new spatial concept for each of his productions.

The influence of Artaud's ideas is very clearly discernible also in the work of three Latin-American directors active in France: Jorge Lavelli, Jerome Savary and Victor Garcia. The last-named, for example, used swivelling seats for a production of Arrabal's *Le Cimetière de Voitures* in Paris some years ago and made the action take place all around the spectators who, at times, were furiously rotating in their seats. Lavelli is a master of magical effects of sound and light. Savary's *Grand Magic Circus* combines elements of circus and ritual, fiction and reality very much in the spirit of Artaud.

The American avantgarde theatre also owes many impulses to Artaud, notably in the work of Judith Malina's and Julian Beck's *Living Theatre*, Joseph Chaikin's *Open Theatre* and Richard Schechner's *Performance Group*. They too reject conventional theatrical space and rely on a maximum of physical expressiveness as against the spoken word, the direct impact on the spectator of events which might be real or fictional, improvisation, audience involvement, etc. Whether Peter Schumann's giant puppets in his work with the Bread and Puppet Theatre are indebted to Artaud rather than Central European folk festivals, these striking and beautiful super-marionettes certainly correspond to Artaud's ideas.

Among the younger generation in France, Ariane Mnouj-kine's *Théâtre du Soleil* with its conception of multi-focused spectacles in an unstructured space where the audience freely moves from one area of action to another clearly owes an immense debt to Artaud, notably with *1789* and *1793* and *L'Age d'Or*. And after his expulsion from the Odéon Jean-Louis Barrault too showed himself willing to use some of the ideas of his old companion-in-arms when performing his spectacle based on Rabelais in a circus, and later when converting the Gare d'Orsay into a wholly original space for theatrical performance.

In Italy Luca Ronconi brilliantly translated Artaudian concepts into theatrical reality with his *Orlando Furioso*, another spectacle staged in an unstructured space in which the ingenious use of moveable rostra created a multitude of different stages and acting areas with the audience freely milling around among giant puppets of horses and knights-in-arms jousting and battling, while weird fairy-tale monsters flew through the air and giant dragons were cut in half. Here Artaud's view that his kind of theatre, far from being an esoteric game for aesthetes and intellectuals, should become a true folk spectacle like the circus and the music hall can be said to have found spectacular justification and confirmation. The same applies to Ronconi's daring and original adaptation of several plays by Aristophanes, *Utopia*, in which trucks and motor cars and even an aeroplane moving in procession through a space shaped like a road create a wholly original multifocal stage which makes the show pass before the audience like a Renaissance *triomfo*.

And, finally, Artaud's postulate that the theatre should merge with real life to form a genuine *event* has no doubt played its part in inspiring and influencing the movement towards a new form — the Happening. In spite of some spectacular successes this still seems to be in its very early stages of development. But its potential and prospects seem far-reaching, provided that, as Artaud had always demanded, genuine poets of genius can be found to put their imagination and creative power into its service.

That Artaud's theoretical writings have borne fruit is, without doubt, evident from this brief and selective account of some of the theatrical ventures that owe him a debt. Whether these or any others that might yet follow in their wake will, in fact, transform human sensibility and consciousness to such a degree that a new theatre will lead to a transformed society and world is another question which only time can answer.

What is however clear even now is that outside the theatre itself Artaud's concepts are strangely gaining in relevance: for example, Artaud's postulate that theatre and life should merge, that a police raid on a brothel was, in some sense, the perfect ballet-like theatrical happening, has been met, not in the theatre, but in the documentary cinema and, above all, in the electronic mass media, radio and television, in which reality is used as the raw material for a dramatically structured presentation of life.

Artaud, who earned most of his living through acting in films, had a highly ambivalent attitude towards the cinema. He clearly saw its potential as an art form using images of the real world; his own film scenario of a Surrealistic sequence of images, *La Coquille et le Clergyman*, shows his understanding of the language of moving pictures. But his disappointment about the way in which Germaine Dulac had directed that film and his experiences with the commercial directors for whom he worked thoroughly disillusioned him and led him, eventually, to hate it. His experience with radio in the last months of his life proved equally disillusioning.

Nevertheless the electronic mass-media and the cinema are, in fact, the fulfilment of at least part of Artaud's vision. Directors like Godard and Antonioni produce profound metaphysical drama through the use of physical reality, immediate, spontaneous and yet meticulously and deliberately shaped and structured. The seeming inner contradiction between Artaud's insistence on utter reality and spontaneity on the one hand, and the most precise and premeditated artistry on the other, *can* be overcome by the combination of the recording of immediate and spontaneous reality through the camera and its exact and deliberate structuring by editing. And the techniques of television which can record events as they happen and transmit them at the same moment, while immediately structuring them by cutting from one camera to another, as in the televising of sports events, political and religious ritual (church services, coronations) or military actions or street demonstrations, are even more closely in conformity with some of Artaud's visionary theoretical pronouncements.

And, indeed, through these techniques Artaud's insistence that Theatre is the double of Life, and Life the double of Theatre, has increasingly been vindicated. More and more in our time, while the theatre (or drama, of which the theatre is only one special case) is increasingly striving towards becoming more closely linked with Life (as in the Happenings movement or theatre in the round), Life is becoming increasingly theatricalised. The theatre is becoming more and more political and politics more and more theatrical.

Artaud's visions which seemed the fantasies of a visionary in the 1930s can now be seen as having been truly prophetic.

And what is an authentic madman? It is a man who has preferred to go mad, in the sense in which society understands the term, rather than be false to a certain superior idea of human honour. That is why society has had all those of whom it wanted to rid itself, against whom it wanted to defend itself, because they had refused to become its accomplices in certain acts of supreme filthiness, condemned to be strangled in its asylums. For a madman is also a man to whom society did not want to listen and whom it wanted to prevent from uttering unbearable truths. (*OCXIII*, *17*)

That is how Artaud, in his impassioned defence of van Gogh which was also a strong plea for his own cause, raised the question which to this day, thirty years later, is a subject of heated and urgent debate, the question as to the true nature of madness and society's attitude to it; and above all the controversy about the function of the psychiatrist. After nine years in a variety of asylums Artaud had strong views on that subject: 'It is almost impossible to be a doctor and an honest man at the same time, but it is damned impossible to be a psychiatrist without at the same time being tarred by the brush of the most indisputable madness: that of being unable to fight that ancient, atavistic mob reflex which makes any scientist in the grip of the mob a born, a congenital enemy of all genius' (*OCXIII*, *31*). But while he proclaimed that it was medicine which had created disease and that psychiatrists were determined to exterminate all men of genius, he also, in the same strange piece of prose, half essay, half poem, returned to the conviction he had nursed through the years of his confinement, that the real cause of his suffering, and that of other kindred spirits of genius, had been occult, a vast conspiracy to put a spell on him and his like: 'That is why unanimous spells were cast on Baudelaire, Edgar Poe, Gérard de Nerval, Nietzsche, Kierkegaard, Hoelderlin, Coleridge, and also van Gogh. It can happen by day, but by preference it happens generally in the night' (*OCXIII, 18*).

And yet Artaud himself was conscious of the fact that notions like that of being bewitched or put under a spell were, in some sense, no more than poetic metaphors: 'What, after all, is a poet' he wrote to one of the psychiatrists at Rodez in January 1945, 'if not a man who visualises and concretises his ideas and his images more intensely and with more telling appropriateness than other people, and gives them, through the rhythm of language, the character of fact' (*OCXI, 11*).

And if, at times, he became violent, was that not understandable in his situation? In defending van Gogh and trying to explain his suicide as the effect of the treatment he had received from society, Artaud made the point: 'I have myself spent nine years in a lunatic asylum and have never suffered from the obsession of wanting to kill myself; but I know that each conversation with a psychiatrist, in the morning, made me want to hang myself because I knew I could not strangle him' (*OCXIII, 38*).

Yet from the very beginning of his career as a writer and man of the theatre Artaud not only knew, but prided himself, that he was suffering from a nervous or psychological ailment, that he was a *case* of outstanding interest. His dependence on, and attachment to, psychiatrists like Dr Toulouse and Dr Allendy shows that he felt himself in need of help, if only to cure his persistent headaches and his difficulties in putting his thoughts on paper. The correspondence with Rivière in which he meticulously describes these difficulties as amounting to a loss of personality, a loss of the sense of existing at all, indicates that his trouble lay deeper than mere migraine. His abortive attempt to have himself psychoanalysed by Dr Allendy also bears this out.

In fact, the knowledge that he was different from other people, that he was destined to suffer, became a vital part of his sense of identity. It was this aspect of his personality – the essay on van Gogh clearly shows this – which enabled him to regard himself as a member of that select band of *poetès maudits* and philosophers like Baudelaire, Nerval, Poe, Nietzsche, Kierkegaard, Hoelderlin and Coleridge (though he finally rejected Coleridge and wrote an essay on 'Coleridge the traitor' in which he denounced him, who had once been a great poet and dreamer of opium dreams, for having killed his own soul to live the life of a bourgeois). And as he never saw himself as, never wanted to be, a run-of-the-mill, *normal* human being, as he was proud of his separateness, his claim to be exceptional, in fact a genius, the issue between Artaud and society never really amounted to a debate whether he was 'mad' or not (if madness merely implied an exceptional psychological make-up, different and remote from drab 'normality') but merely whether society was entitled to incarcerate him for nine years under abominable conditions which, for most of the time, amounted to calculated brutality and torture. And if, during part of that period, he suffered from violent tantrums or withdrawal symptoms of an extreme nature, was that not due to the shock he had suffered when he was suddenly clapped into a straitjacket and imprisoned? If, as was undoubtedly the case, this sudden arrest was due to his having caused a disturbance in the streets of Dublin, and then, on the *Washington*, having attacked the men who entered his cabin, the cause of Artaud's violent behaviour was clearly no more than an unfortunate misunderstanding arising from his inability to grasp questions addressed to him in a foreign language. Apart from this his behaviour, before his confinement, though odd, had never been a menace to society. He might have paraded through the Latin Quarter of Paris brandishing his miraculous cane and striking sparks from the pavement with its metal point while uttering loud prophetic curses. But that had never done anyone any harm.

Of course, the decisions to go to Mexico and, even more so, to set out on the journey to Ireland in a state of apocalyptic exaltation could hardly be described as outstandingly rational acts. Yet had not society, in its refusal to give him an opportunity to realise his artistic ideas without compromising his integrity, literally driven him out into the wilderness? But on the other hand was not this rejection and the martyrdom of confinement as a lunatic, in a higher sense, the only way in which he could fully realise his destiny and establish the identity which made him the adored idol of posterity? These are questions which are truly unanswerable, as unanswerable as the question, *mutatis mutandis*, whether Pontius Pilate and Judas Iscariot should be blamed for having caused the Crucifixion or praised for having enabled the divine plan to be fulfilled.

Be that as it may, Artaud's preoccupation with his own predicament, his lucidity even in periods of extreme mental tension, and his genius as a writer have made his story one of the best-documented case histories of all time, on a par with the writings of the Marquis de Sade or Daniel Paul Schreber. The brilliance with which he described his writing difficulties and the spontaneity of his utterances in his last years which allow profound and immediate insights into the workings of the deepest recesses of the human psyche probably make Artaud's oeuvre even more valuable than that of these classics of human self-revelation.

The first question which Artaud's case raises is that of the organic origin of his nervous disability. Whether or not the supposed attack from meningitis from which he suffered at the age of five really was, as is often assumed, the source of all his troubles, he repeatedly mentioned that since the age of six he had undergone periods of stuttering, nervous contractions of the facial muscles and the tongue, and later

> spasms of pain in the right side of the neck which cut my breathing . . . limbs which become numb and begin to prickle, violent itching which suddenly moves from the arms to the legs, the spinal column full of crackles, painful on top. A violent weakness, ready to drop to the ground, which is an amplification of the unbearable compression of the head and the shoulderblades. At times a general cramp which comes and goes, at others all the feelings of intense fever : cramp, heat, shivering, droning noises in the ears, pain caused by light. (*OCI Suppl.*, 89-90)

In the letter to Dr Allendy in which he gives this catalogue of ailments, dated 22 March 1929, Artaud makes a special point of assuring the doctor that all these symptoms had appeared although he had stopped taking drugs weeks ago. If these, however, *were* withdrawal symptoms, it must be remembered that he had started to take laudanum ten years earlier precisely because he had been advised that it would stop these physical discomforts. Or could all these symptoms have had a psychological origin ?

In another long letter describing his disability to the acupuncturist Soulié de Morant, in February 1932, Artaud categorically stated that his physical symptoms had been 'complicated by psychological troubles which only appeared *in a spectacular fashion* at the age of nineteen' (*OCI Suppl.*, 130). This was the time, when, as he told Jean Hort, he had destroyed all his youthful writings and given his books away to his friends. It was the onset of this depression which led to his first stay at a sanatorium. And it is also the exact moment when the incident of his being stabbed by a pimp, which he dwelt on a great deal in his period of confinement, is supposed to have happened.

What kind of psychological trauma could Artaud have suffered in his adolescence? 'Until my twenty-seventh year' he said in a lecture in Mexico in 1936,

> I lived with an obscure hatred of the Father, and of my own father in particular. To the day I saw him die. Then that inhuman severity with which I accused him of treating me, suddenly ceased. Another being emerged from that body. And for the first time in my life my father stretched out his arm towards me. And I, who suffer from unease in my body, understood that he had suffered unease in his body and that there is a lie in existence against which we are born to protest. (OCVIII, 178)

Another traumatic event in his early life to which he often referred was the death of his infant sister Germaine, aged seven months, when he was not yet nine years old. While it would be vain to speculate on the nature of possible feelings of guilt about this event, it is certainly striking that the subject which most attracted him in the theatre was that of incest: in the early playlet, Le Jet de Sang, there is a scene of incest between a young man and his sister, followed by a series of horribly disgusting erotic images of old women. Artaud's only detailed analysis of a play which he introduced as an example of The Theatre of Cruelty in The Theatre and its Double is that of John Ford's 'Tis Pity she's a Whore, also involving incest between brother and sister; and The Cenci describes the incestuous rape of a daughter by her father, followed by the horrible murder of the guilty parent. In the years of his confinement when he was drawing up lists of the women he had most loved in his life, Artaud always called these his daughters, even though they usually included his two grandmothers, the sisters Neneka and Catherine Schili.

The element of sexual guilt feelings also strongly emerges from his violent refusal to admit any suggestion that he might be suffering from the after-effects of syphilis. Shortly after his arrival at Rodez he wrote to one of the doctors, pointing out that the fact that his pupils were unequal could not possibly imply that he might himself have contracted syphilis 'because I do not know and despise all sexual relations of whatever kind as being degrading for man and it is therefore a grave insult to me for anyone to believe that my body could ever have indulged in these at any moment in my life' (*OCX, 13*). He went on to complain bitterly that because the inequality of his pupils had been taken for an indication that he suffered from the after-effects of syphilis, which must be hereditary, he had ever since 1917 been subjected to an endless succession of injections with substances ranging from mercury to novarsenobenzole which had greatly aggravated his nervous condition.

Artaud's total rejection of all sex from the period of the collapse of his theatrical hopes onward, which led to his elaboration of a complete mythology about God having created man without sexual and digestive organs and his belief that man had been degraded into a sexual and defecating being by the intervention of evil extra-terrestrial forces (a belief which he maintained even after he had again abandoned the fervent Christianity to which he had been converted before his transfer to Rodez) also point to a regression to an early period of violent sexual guilt. In some of his writings towards the end of his life he went so far as to deny ever having owed his own life to a sexual act between his parents: 'I, Antoine Artaud, I am my son, my father, my mother . . .' (*OCXII, 77*).

> *Je ne crois à ni père*
> *ni mère*
> *je na pas*
> *a papa-mama*

(I believe in neither father/nor mother/I have not papa-mama) (*OCXII, 99*).

The violent rage, 'the fury which has been rising in me for 49 years' (*OCIX, 193*) as he called it when he was forty-nine years old, is another aspect of Artaud's personality which points to deep pent-up guilt feelings and frustrations translating themselves into aggressiveness. The concept of the

Theatre of Cruelty through which mankind was to be shaken out of its complacency and contentment and to be made aware of the depth of emotion and suffering beneath the calm surface of its life, could well, in the last analysis, be regarded as a violent assault against humanity as a whole.

There is also a link between Artaud's aggressiveness against a world unaware of his mental and physical torments and the whole complex of drug addiction which eventually became one of the main inner motivations of his elaborate gnostic mythology. In a document dating from the beginnings of his association with the Surrealists, which was published on 1 January 1925, Artaud made an impassioned plea for the free use of opium as the only possible remedy for a long list of sufferers, including 'lucid madmen, tabetics, cancer patients and those afflicted with chronic meningitis' whom he addressed, with obvious fellow feeling:

> you are outside life, you are above life, you are afflicted with ills the ordinary person does not know, you transcend the normal level and that is what people hold against you, you poison their quietude, you corrode their stability. You feel repeated and fugitive pain, insoluble pain, pain outside thought, pain which is neither in the body, nor the mind, but which partakes of both. And I, who share your ills, I am asking: who should dare to restrict the means that bring us relief? (*OCVIII*, 25)

Artaud used to emphasise at this period of his life that he did not resort to opium and similar drugs because of the pleasures of intoxication, but simply as a relief from pain, as a medicine he needed to enable him to work. In a text which remained unpublished at the time but on which he was working in 1934 he stressed that it was 'a state outside life' – the loss of the sense of self from which he had suffered from puberty – 'which made me one day resort to opium. I have not been able to get rid of it and never shall' (*OCVIII*, 25). And, although he regarded opium as an 'abominable swindle' he needed it, though 'it is not opium which enables me to work, but its absence; and to feel its absence it must from time to time pass through me' (*OCVIII*, 26). In the same fragment Artaud provides an insight into the effect of his disability – and of opium – on his sexuality: 'Virility is intermittent . . . everything comes in periods. At times there is the sensuality of a Mammoth . . . at others the sufferer is an angel, a priest, a pitiful sacristan' (*OCVIII*, 27). It is surely significant that later, when he was constructing his anti-sex mythology, Artaud claimed that his body had been invaded by an angel.

The vast conspiracy of 'initiates' who, he believed in his years of confinement, had put him under a terrible spell was, among other things, concerned with denying him access to opium. The intoxicating power of opium itself, he explained in his letters from Rodez, was the result of a spell that had been put upon it, while its real object was to make exceptional souls able to transcend themselves. The English had put Chaucer and Joan of Arc to death and had conducted an opium war in China for that very reason, 'because they are whites, and opium is black and they wanted to exterminate the black' (*OCIX*, 204).

Just as what had initially been mere anger with the authorities who made access to drugs difficult grew and intensified itself in Artaud's mind into a world conspiracy to deny him opium, so his sense of pride in being separated from others by his disability, his suffering, magnified itself first into the image of the Tortured Man of the tarot pack who was to bring deliverance to mankind in *Les Nouvelles Révélations de l'Etre*, and later became the conviction that it was he, Artaud, who had been crucified on Golgotha :

I was on Golgotha two thousand years ago and my name was, as always, Artaud, and I detested the priests and God, and that was why I was crucified by the priests of Jehovah, as a poet and an enlightened one, and then thrown on a heap of dung . . . I know that filthy little swine, that terrible little spell-caster of Judaea whom all of today's Christianity adores, and who had himself accepted as resurrected in the light under the name of Jesus-Christ. When in fact he was none other than a certain M. Nalpas . . . (*OCIX*, 204)

It must be remembered that until shortly before he wrote this text Artaud had insisted on signing all his letters with his mother's maiden-name, Nalpas, and had also been excessively pious and assiduous in observing all the rites of the Catholic Church. So *both* his selves claimed to be Jesus Christ.

Violent oscillation of attitudes between extremes is characteristic of Artaud's fantasy life in his last phase. His attitude to sexuality swung from identification with Heliogabalus, that secular incarnation of sexual excess and depravity, to a total, disgusted rejection of sex. The revolutionary, who had wanted to use the theatre to subvert the existing structure of the bourgeois state, assured Paulhan in 1943 that 'Religion, Family and Fatherland are the three things I respect . . . I have always been a royalist and patriot' (*OCX*, 103-4), and even dedicated a copy of *Les Nouvelles Révélations de l'Etre* to Hitler. He became exceedingly pious and later exceedingly blasphemous. Having been a devoted disciple of the Cabbala and Oriental religions, he later became convinced that it was in fact the Jews and the Lamas of Tibet who were casting their spells upon him. The image which rationalised these violent changes in his attitudes was that of one self having died while another occupied, or usurped the body. He applied the same reasoning to his friends : those who had disappointed him were no longer the same people but zombies whose bodies were inhabited by evil spirits.

After his release from Rodez Artaud continued to believe in the conspiracy that had put him under a spell. But at the same time, by another characteristic reversal of attitudes, his aggression was now mainly directed against Dr Ferdière, whom he had still assured of his devotion and gratitude on the train journey to Paris, and psychiatrists and doctors in general.

As his body was increasingly racked by cancer Artaud developed another fascinating dissociation : his aggression turned against his own body. In one of his late poems he accuses the evil, earth-bound God of the Gnostics, the Demiurge, of having usurped his body because he could

> find no better way
>   to achieve being
> than to be born at the price
>   of my assassination.[1]

Yet, at the same time, he who had so deeply believed in the mission of the body as the seat of emotion through which life realises itself to the full found a way to reconcile that conviction with a violent *hatred* of the body. He developed the belief that while the body, seat of feeling and sensation, was of immense value, it could do without organs, which, far from making up the body, destroy its unity by hurting and constantly obtruding their own obscene individuality. Man's anatomy, Artaud demanded in the concluding section of his radio programme, must be completely re-made, for:

> . . . there is nothing so useless as an organ.
> Once you have given Man a body without organs,
> you will have delivered him from all his automatisms
> and given him back his true freedom. (*OCXIII, 104*)

There is a significant analogy between Artaud's dissociation of the body and its organs and Beckett's limbless heroes who have shed some of their organs in the pursuit of their real self.

By another and analogous dissociation Artaud, more than ever disgusted by sex and defecation, the organs of which he detested more than any others, used increasingly scatological and obscene language in attacking them. And this disgust with the organs of the body eventually turned into a disgust with existence itself:

> Where there is a stink of shit
> there is a smell of being. (*OCXIII, 83*)

That rage against his disability which deprived him of his sense of being in his youth was now transmuted into a fervent wish to be liberated from the pain and distress of being itself.

This brief attempt to list and describe some of the aspects of Artaud's psychological development is neither an analysis nor does it want to be anything like a diagnosis of his case. There are those who have categorised it as schizophrenia, paraphrenia, paranoia, or religious mania, whether inborn, acquired by physical lesions in early youth or caused by society's rejection, or, indeed, by psychiatric treatment itself in mental hospitals. Others have seen it as a poet's exaltation and inspired frenzy which enabled him to provide unique insights into human nature. One or another of these views, or, indeed, several, may be true.

What is beyond doubt is that the history of Artaud's psyche, so fully and so eloquently documented, has given considerable impulses to the thinking of our time in the field of psychology, psychoanalysis and their social applications. Important seminal works like Michel Foucault's *Histoire de la Folie* and Deleuze and Guattari's *L'Anti-Oedipe* make considerable use of insights derived from Artaud, as does the work of R. D. Laing and his associates.

None of the disabilities, fantasies and structures of myth which Artaud produced are in themselves perhaps very different from those of many other sufferers from similarly distressing states of mind. But his genius as a writer, his eloquence and descriptive brilliance contribute a great deal to the impact and paradigmatic quality of his case. And here again a further, and mysterious element enters in: what really gives this highly particular and personal case truly universal significance, is again, ultimately, Artaud's achievement in wholly *living*, totally incarnating his experience. In that sense he may have been very near the truth when he claimed that he was being crucified to bear the burden of all mankind. His pain, distress and torment certainly produced an intensity of psychic energy which can still make itself felt in the fervour it continues to inspire and to generate.

6 Irrationalism, Aggression, Revolution

During the night of 16 May 1968 crowds of insurgent Paris students flooded into the Odéon-Théâtre de France, then under the artistic direction of Jean-Louis Barrault, and occupied the venerable old building. As the first of the revolutionary youths burst into Barrault's office and saw the portrait of Artaud above his desk, he exclaimed: '*Il a volé Artaud!*' (He has stolen Artaud!)[1].

That young revolutionary who had never known Artaud almost certainly had no idea that Barrault had been Artaud's comrade-in-arms, had shared many of his most intimate thoughts, had been his friend and disciple, had responded to his appeals for help in the dark years of his confinement and was continuing Artaud's work in the theatre. To the student revolutionary *that* Artaud did not exist. For him Artaud was the embodiment of his own rejection of society as constituted in 1968, the scourge of the bourgeoisie, the source of a stream of invective and abuse against established institutions. An abstract image of Artaud had swamped the real Artaud, whom Jean-Louis Barrault had known and loved, and was now floating ahead of the teeming masses of rioting young people, a lodestar of their revolt.

Artaud's *Lettre aux Recteurs des Universités Européennes* (Letter to the Chancellors of Europe's Universities), which had formed part of Number Three of *La Révolution Surréaliste* (April 1925), had been one of the first leaflets issued by the students of the Sorbonne in May 1968. And although this text, as we now know, was not entirely written by Artaud, being a collaborative effort of the Surrealist movement, it made him one of the chief inspirations of the student revolt. It fitted its spirit to perfection:

> Europe crystallises and slowly mummifies under the chains of its frontiers, its factories, its law courts, its universities. The frozen Spirit cracks under the slabs of stone which press upon it. It's the fault of your mouldy systems, your logic of two and two makes four, it is your

fault, University Chancellors, caught in the nets of your own syllogisms. You produce engineers, judges, doctors unable to grasp the true mysteries of the body, the cosmic laws of being, false scientists blind to the world beyond the Earth, philosophers who pretend they can reconstruct the Spirit . . . Leave us alone, gentlemen, you are nothing but usurpers. By what right do you pretend to canalise intelligence, to award diplomas of the Spirit? (*OCI*, 335-6)

Shortly after Artaud, as a member of the Surrealist movement, had produced this and other equally aggressively denunciatory letters to the Pope, the Dalai Lama and the Schools of Buddha he broke with the Surrealists precisely because they had decided to translate their revolutionary attitude into action by joining the Communist Party, while Artaud obstinately maintained that political action was useless and true revolution could only come by a transformation of the human consciousness and spirit from within. Convinced as he was throughout his life – this is the one strand of total consistency that runs through his *oeuvre* – that it was the spirit of rationalism, analytic and discursive thought, formal logic and linguistic pedantry which had desiccated the fullness of Man's emotional life and cut him off from the profound sources of his vital being, Artaud rejected revolutionary Marxism as simply another form of rationalism. 'The Communist revolution ignores the inner world of thought' (*OCVIII, 191*) he declared in one of his lectures in Mexico (1936); European civilisation had to be rejected because of its rationalism:

To find its profound nature again, to feel itself live in its thought, Life rejects the spirit of analysis in which Europe has gone astray. Poetic knowledge is internal, the poetic quality is internal. There is a movement today which aims at identifying the poetry of the poets with the magical inner force which carves a way for Life and allows us to have an influence on Life. Whether thought is a secretion of matter or not – I don't want to spend time on discussing the question. I shall simply say that the materialism of Lenin seems in fact to ignore this poetics of thought. (*OCVIII, 192*)

Hence 'the revolution invented by Marx is a caricature of

Life' (*OCVIII*, *184*). In notes for another lecture or article for Mexico he put the matter even more succinctly : 'Have come to Mexico/to flee Barbarity of Europe/last example of European Barbarity : Marxism' (*OCVIII*, *157*).

The student revolutionaries of 1968 – and the adherents to the contemporary new revolutionary counter-culture which reached its peak around 1970 and has been on the wane since the mid-1970s – also rejected Marxism in its rationalist and 'scientific' guise, hence Artaud's image of an anti-rationalist, drug-addicted mystic and visionary believer in the Cabbala, the tarot and Eastern religions was particularly attractive and potent for them. To fashion that image they had to fuse elements from his thought and writings from different periods of his career into a highly unhistorical amalgam : taking quotations from texts from a period when Artaud *did* believe in the Cabbala and the Tibetan Book of the Dead, they had to ignore his vehement denunciation of mysticism and Oriental cults during a later period from which, however, even more violent denunciations of established civilisation (like the nightmare of schoolboys' sperm being deep-frozen for the future production of American cannon-fodder) admirably served the anti-American *zeitgeist*. Yet, undoubtedly, the chief appeal of Artaud for the revolutionary counter-culture was the vehemence of his denunciations, whatever the target at which they were directed, the violence of his vituperative rhetoric.

It is as though Artaud's pent-up frustrations which had exploded in writing of unparalleled aggressiveness retained their power beyond the grave and were able to engender and energise aggressive forces of a similar nature across space and time. So great were the psychic energies stored in Artaud's brilliantly-written poetic outbursts, so powerful was his style, so potent his expressive force that, like the initial release of energy in an atomic bomb, they were able to unleash a veritable chain-reaction in the minds of countless individuals who in turn inspired similar aggressive sentiments in scores of others they encountered on their paths.

Ironically enough, all those who knew him intimately agree that in his personal life Artaud was an exceptionally mild, sweet-natured man. All the more powerfully, it seems, did his suppressed aggressions issue into his writings. Only in one sphere, that of the theatre, was he ever concerned in propounding a *positive* vision : his proposals may in some respects have been impractical or difficult to implement, but they were constructive and amounted to an alternative blue-print. But when it came to denounce the iniquities of the contemporary established social order and culture, Artaud's denunciation was purely negative. He denounced industrial civilisation, with its machines, science, medicine, the pedantries of the law; but all he could advocate to replace it was a vague desire to return to the Middle Ages, ancient Mexican civilisation or – at certain points in his career – the supposedly happier life-styles of ancient China or Tibet. Such preponderance of negative over positive ideas, however, was also the hall-mark of the new counter-culture. It is, after all, inherent in any irrational or anti-rational attitude that a rational thinking-out of the tactics and aims of the movement would be a contradiction in terms and would re-introduce the self-same analytical method which it is its aim to transcend. Let the old order crumble and be swept away and the sweetness and light of a new utopia will instantly, as if by *magic*, be re-stored! Hence the emphasis on magic in Artaud's anticipation of a great cosmic upheaval at the time of his adventure with St Patrick's cane. The revolutionary movement of 1968 acted on very similar principles. Its adherents also believed in the release of spontaneous creative forces (which, to a certain degree, actually occurred) and a transformation of society by these creative energies (which did not occur).

The danger of such a surrender to the Dionysiac life force and its creative ecstasy lies in the blindness of such raptures. It is energy without a defined direction or aim, and ultimately might lead to violence as an end in itself.

Artaud, always the complete incarnation of his own thought, exemplifies precisely these dangers in a paradigmatic fashion. During the war Artaud dedicated a copy of his *Nouvelles Révélations de l'Etre* to Hitler (another believer in the right of the individual to follow his inspiration, however violent) and his aggressiveness was directed against vast conspiracies of Jews, Jesuits, British Secret Service agents and other favourite targets of the political lunatic fringe of the Right as well as the Left. The violent anti-Americanism of his last broadcast was simply a direct continuation of the same tendency to look for an explanation of history in secret societies and wicked conspiracies. On 6 August 1947 Artaud told Jacques Prevel that 'seven to eight hundred million human beings . . .

should be exterminated; what is that to the three or four thousand million who inhabit the earth. Most human beings spend their life in doing nothing, exploiting the life of others, taking hold of their consciousness . . .'[2]

Blind aggressiveness on this scale, albeit only in the mind of a dying poet indulging luxuriant day-dreams, is closely akin to the ideologies that were realised in the genocide perpetrated by the totalitarian rulers of our time, whether on the Left or the Right, Fascist, Nazi or Communist. In the ambivalence of his blind aggressiveness Artaud incarnated and anticipated the ultimate absence of distinction between such labels and ideological colours in the face of destruction on that scale. Whether, in his confinement at Rodez, he was claiming that Breton, the Surrealist who had led his movement into the bosom of the Communist Party, had fought to free him from arrest at the quayside of Le Havre side by side with battalions of the extreme Right-wing *Action Française* against a Jewish-controlled French police force, or whether denouncing the whole of Western, bourgeois culture, surely a Right-wing phenomenon, as doomed to utter destruction, Artaud was merely letting his frustration, rage and destructive fervour flow regardless of ideology into any channel that seemed to offer itself by the chance of the moment. And that, of necessity, is where a cult of emotion for emotion's sake, provided it is deeply felt and of maximum intensity, and wholly untrammelled by thought, must ultimately lead.

In their brilliant, but highly disturbing study of capitalism and schizophrenia which fuses Freudianism and Marxism on a structuralist basis, *L'Anti-Oedipe*, Gilles Deleuze and Felix Guattari derive much of their argumentation from the case history and personality of Artaud whom they regard both as a paradigmatic, well-documented *case* and as a kind of saintly *model*. To them society is at present polarised between the capitalist-Fascist attitude, gregarious, rejoicing in large numbers and participation in a superior race or nation, which corresponds to the clinical picture of *paranoia* on the one hand; and on the other, the revolutionary attitude, which is that of an isolated, despised outcast, cut off from the crowd, withdrawing into his inner self which presents the phenotype of *schizophrenia*. But if the revolutionary in his hatred of organised society develops his aggressiveness against it to fever pitch and if, as Deleuze and Guattari clearly advocate, the revolutionaries unite in concerted action against society, then, surely, schizophrenia has itself become paranoia and the revolutionary attitude is merely the reverse side of the medal which has Fascism on its obverse. Deleuze and Guattari explicitly recognise that 'the two poles are united in Artaud's magic formula: Heliogabalus – the anarchist'.[3] And, indeed, Artaud exemplifies the profound identity of all political attitudes based on the primacy of emotion over reason and their inevitable resort to violently aggressive action.

The use made of Artaud's image in France and elsewhere by a wide variety of different movements and causes clearly illustrates this state of affairs. In France, whose cultural life has long been dominated by a philosophy of sweet reasonableness, a fine balance between emotion and the intellect, a belief in the middle way, self-control and action based on logic, Artaud's rejection of the Apollonian principle in favour of the unrestrained ecstasies of Dionysos, has rallied a whole generation eager to reject the traditions of a past which has gone stale and become boring. The example of Artaud is to them a welcome model; it shows that emotion released from all restraint of logic, from any need to seek empirical endorsement of its conclusions, can result in a glorious rhetoric of unbridled passion. Much of what goes by the name of philosophy or political science in France today is, basically, just such Artaudian rhetoric, words used for their emotional charge, even the mere sensuous impact of their sound rather than their meaning. That Artaud's writings, oscillating as they do between the most contradictory positions, enable him to be quoted at will in support of any emotional or 'ideological' stance, is another important point in their favour. Orthodox Catholics can use him as readily as Maoists: there is a delicious essay proving that Artaud and Mao Tse-tung are ultimately one in the volume chronicling the proceedings of a symposium on Artaud, held by the *Tel Quel* group in 1972. The argument is simple: Artaud liked the Orient; China is in the Orient; Mao Tse-tung is Chinese – ergo Artaud is a Maoist.[4] Similarly Artaud, who at times denounced opium as a pernicious and evil thing, at others clamoured for it, has become one of the chief idols of the American drug-culture. Even Artaud's concept that the theatre should merge into life and life become theatre was clearly present in the American counter-culture's tactics of turning street violence or the conduct of a trial like that of the Chicago Seven into theatrical Happenings, street and court room *theatre*.

To record the fact that Artaud and his writings have engendered, or have served as a pretext for engendering, violence is not to say that he is to be blamed for that violence, or, indeed, for the flood of stupidities which are proclaimed by would-be disciples. Here too Artaud's fate is that of all those Masters whose message is incarnated in their life rather than in a coherent body of work. The image, or fragments of the image, become detached from the personality as an organic whole, and assume a life of their own. As Artaud postulated it for the theatre, so also a powerful image releases emotions, body sensations, in those who are exposed to it; but who can tell what those emotions will amount to, in what action they may result? The beauty of Artaud, the monk ministering to St Joan on the stake may engender devotion; the ravaged features of Artaud, the martyr of Rodez, may arouse pity and anger at the society who made him suffer; but once those emotions are transformed into energies of belief or action, they may well be far removed from what Artaud himself felt, thought and stood for. Precisely because Artaud's ideas are totally incarnated in Artaud's life and personality, they only make sense in the context of his own experience, above all his own suffering. His rage and aggressiveness are, ultimately, merely poetic metaphors for his suffering and can only be understood as complementary to it. *He* had the right to utter those heart-rending screams of pain we can still hear in his last recording, because he suffered the pain from which they sprang. But that does not give others, who have not felt that pain, the justification to start uttering equally loud and strident cries. Without the suffering such screams are hollow, empty, superficial and a fake. And what is true of the screams is equally true of violent talk and violent action. The middle-class student revolutionaries of the Paris riots of May 1968 who used Artaud's aggressiveness to power their own frustrations did not share these sufferings and, ultimately, merely exploited them for their own shallow ends and to provide cheap thrills for themselves. In that sense, they, not Jean-Louis Barrault, had stolen Artaud.

7   Conclusion

Antonin Artaud, the man who lived and suffered and raged and was loved by his friends, is dead. He no longer exists. But the residue of his existence – a million words in a long row of collected writings and letters; his drawings; the shape of his body still moving in his films; the strident tones of his voice on the tapes he recorded – all that not only exists but is still alive and active. And like that corpse in Ionesco's play which keeps on growing, Artaud's remains also are still expanding: around his own *oeuvre* there accumulate the reminiscences of those who knew him, the commentaries and explanations, the tracts which exhort this or that group or type of his followers and disciples to emulate his actions or to live by his image and example.

Most people, when they die, leave something behind – possessions, memories, writings; but these gradually fade away and lose their impact. Even the work of important thinkers or scientists is gradually absorbed into the general stream of established knowledge and, by becoming commonplace, gradually dissolves the individuality and personal influence of the men themselves. The cases in which the *personality* rather than the *oeuvre* or achievement of an important figure continues to increase in its impact are very rare. Only the founders of religions can genuinely claim such powerful and expanding potency. Artaud was not – or has at least not *yet* become – the founder of a religion. But he has become the centre of a cult, or, indeed, several cults. And as such he has something in common with the founders of religions. As he did not aim to create an *oeuvre* so much as to make his own life his supreme work of art and thus to *incarnate* his ideas rather than merely *express* them, he engenders not the appreciation given to great artists but the devotion due to a beloved individual. And the very contradictoriness, dissociation, even incoherence of his ideas, merely strengthens such primarily emotional devotion, which must ultimately lead to a cult. An ideology can be disproved and discredited. A work of poetry, painting or music can be criticised, but a *person* can merely be loved or rejected. And those who love such a personality love him with all his contradictions. The presence of the personality however, its continued presence, is ensured by the intensity of the psychic energy enshrined in the manifestations of its activity which have remained with posterity. And Artaud not only had that exceptional potency of psychic energy, he also had the gift to project it in a fashion which is more than merely supreme artistic craftsmanship, which, indeed, in the spontaneity and directness which puts it beyond the bounds of merely aesthetic analysis as art, is akin to magic. In this sense Artaud's concept of the theatre is completely vindicated by the manner in which he succeeded in transforming his own life into a dream, his own personality into a unique theatrical character, a character, however, whose sufferings were *real* in the full sense of the word but who was projected to the world by an *actor* who had the supreme skill of transmitting to his audience the strength, intensity and colour of the emotions involved, by a process akin to that vibration of the soil through which the snake-charmer in Artaud's simile imposes his emotion on the coils of the snake's body. The plays Artaud wrote and produced were far from perfect, but his own life was the perfect tragedy, perfectly enacted. That is why its impact continues beyond the grave.

The cults through which Artaud's psychic energy remains intense and active may, in themselves, be silly, shallow or intellectually feeble. This is not to say that one of them may not gradually, as a tradition coagulates around it, turn into a powerful current, become the basis of some sort of religion. History knows examples of this kind of phenomenon.

On a more mundane and secular level, however, Artaud, unlike some other personalities around whom cults have grown up, is unique in the fullness of the documentation he has provided about his life and in the fascinating general implications of his case. In the completeness of his self-revelation he joins the select group of the great masters of that genre which cannot be classed as mere art but is the full presentation of human life experience itself: Pepys, Casanova, the Marquis de Sade, the Marquise de Sévigné, Boswell, Horace Walpole. . . .

Artaud lacks the serenity and inner calm of most of these – the Marquis de Sade is the obvious exception – but, on the other hand, he presents a more extravagantly fascinating psychological – or even psychopathological – case history. He himself saw himself as one of a long line of *poètes maudits*: Hoelderlin, Baudelaire, Nerval, Lautréamont, Nietzsche. And he was undoubtedly right. Yet none of these has left as full and enlightening a documentation about himself as that which Artaud has left to posterity.

But Artaud transcends the category of the *poètes maudits* as well as those of the great self-revealers. For he provides an immense wealth of detailed insights into a human type of the utmost importance in history, a fascinating anachronism in our times, but all the more valuable through the material he furnishes us with about this crucially influential kind of character: the character, that is, of the 'Holy Fool'. It was Artaud's misfortune that he was born into an epoch which consigns individuals of this stamp into lunatic asylums. In other epochs he might have been a shaman, a prophet, an alchemist, an oracle, a saint, a gnostic teacher or, indeed, the founder of a new religion. The intensity of his emotion, the depth of his commitment, the rich flow of his myth-making faculty, the eloquence of his language, his all-powerful urge to create ritual (for that, essentially, was the nature of his fanaticism for the theatre), the terrifying violence of his invective, the grandiose craziness of his exaltation, all these were present in personalities who, in other epochs, were revered, adored and martyred as divinely-inspired or diabolically-possessed vessels of powers transcending the bounds of mere humanity.

Artaud's fate in our time may be a mark of its enlightenment or a disturbing symptom of its spiritual poverty. But whether it is the one or the other, the fate, the martyrdom, the clinical case of Antonin Artaud, *Artaud le Mômo*, the holy fool, is a touchstone of our civilisation.

Notes

1 MASTER OR MADMAN? (pages 9-14)
    1. Jean-Louis Barrault, *Souvenirs pour demain* (Paris, 1972), p. 104.

2 THE ROAD TO RODEZ (pages 15-64)
    1. Letter from Dullin to Blin, *Cahiers de la Compagnie Renaud-Barrault*, No. 22-23 (May, 1958), p. 20.
    2. Jean Hort, *Antonin Artaud, le suicidé de la société* (Geneva, 1960), p. 56.
    3. Antonin Artaud, *Lettres à Genica Athanasiou* (Paris, 1969), p. 208.
    4. *The Journals of Anais Nin*, vol. I (London, 1966), pp. 195-6.
    5. ibid., p. 232.
    6. ibid., pp. 238-9.
    7. ibid., p. 71.
    8. André Frank in *Lettres d'Antonin Artaud à Jean-Louis Barrault* (Paris, 1952), p. 65.
    9. ibid., p. 71.
    10. *The Journals of Anais Nin*, vol. 2 (London, 1968), p. 247.
    11. *Lettres à Genica Athanasiou*, pp. 309-310.
    12. *La Tour de Feu*, No. 63/64 (December, 1959), p. 31.
    13. Ferdière in BBC broadcast.
    14. *La Tour de Feu*, p. 75.
    15. Jacques Prevel, *En compagnie d'Antonin Artaud* (Paris, 1974), p. 113.
    16. André Gide in *Combat*, 19 March 1948, quoted in Jean-Louis Brau, *Antonin Artaud* (Paris, 1971), p. 235.

4 THE ARTAUDIAN THEATRE—
        THEORY AND PRACTICE (pages 76-95)
    1. This is the passage which gave Arrabal the idea for his play, *The Architect and the Emperor of Assyria*.
    2. Artaud's insistence on this high degree of pre-rehearsed and pre-determined precision – the very antithesis of improvisation – seems, as Jacques Derrida has pointed out in a famous essay, '*Le Théâtre de la Cruauté et la clôture de la répresentation*' (included in the volume *L'Ecriture et la Différence*) to be in contradiction with two passages in *The Theatre and its Double* (OCIV, 91, 99) in which Artaud seems to insist on the uniqueness and unrepeatability of each

theatrical event. Derrida links these passages with quotations from Artaud's much later writings in which he denied the possibility of theatre altogether. On closer inspection, however, the passages from *The Theatre and its Double* quoted by Derrida are taken out of context and refer to quite different points; the first one to the unrepeatability of fixed statements such as are contained in recognised classical, but now dead, works; and the second to the irreversibility of actions in *reality* which the theatre, however by sublimating the emotion *can* make repeatable.

3. Jean-Louis Barrault, quoted in Jean-Louis Brau, op. cit., p. 97.
4. 'Le Théâtre et la Science' (1947).
5. December, 1946.
6. 'Le Théâtre de la Cruauté', 19 November 1947.

5 MORE DEVILS THAN VAST HELL CAN HOLD (pages 96-106)
   1. From a poem in *84*, No. 5/6, 1948.

6 IRRATIONALISM, AGGRESSION, REVOLUTION (pages 107-13)
   1. Jean-Louis Brau, op. cit., p. 166n.
   2. Jacques Prevel, op. cit., p. 168.
   3. Gilles Deleuze and Félix Guattari, *L'Anti-Oedipe* (Paris, 1972), p. 330.
   4. Jacques Henric, 'Artaud travaillé par la China' in *Artaud*, ed. Philippe Sollers (Paris, 1973).

Chronology

1896	4 September: 8 a.m.: Antonin Marie Joseph Artaud born at Marseilles, 4, Rue Jardin des Plantes – son of Antoine Roi Artaud and Euphrasie Artaud, née Nalpas.
1901	Artaud suffers an attack of 'meningitis'.
1905	21 August: Death of Artaud's infant sister Germaine (born 13 January 1905).
1906	Artaud almost drowned while staying at Smyrna with his maternal grandmother Mariette (Miette or Neneka) Schili (or Chili, Schily, Chilé).
1910	At his school, the Collège du Sacré Coeur, Artaud starts a literary review and publishes his first poems under the pseudonym Louis des Attides.
1915	In a fit of depression Artaud destroys all his writings and gives away his books. Spends his first period in a sanatorium at La Rougière near Marseilles.
1916	Called up for military service at Digne. Released after nine months on medical grounds.
1916–18	Periods at sanatoria and health resorts: St Dizier near Lyons; Lafoux-les-Bains (Gard); Divonne-les-Bains (Ain).
1918	Stay at Bagnères-de-Bigorre (Pyrénées).
End 1918–1920	At the sanatorium of Le Chanet near Neuchâtel, Switzerland, under the care of Dr Dardel.
1919	May: Begins to take laudanum to relieve headaches.
1920	March: Arrives in Paris where he is put in the care of Dr Edouard Toulouse at Villejuif.
	Begins to collaborate on Dr Toulouse's literary review *Demain*.
	August: *Demain* publishes a poem and an article by Artaud.
	Late autumn: Lugné-Poe offers Artaud a part at the Théâtre de l'Oeuvre.
1921	17 February: First appearance as an actor in a small non-speaking part in *Les Scrupules de Sganarelle* by Henri de Régnier at the Théâtre de l'Oeuvre.
	October: Through his uncle Louis Nalpas, artistic director of the Société des Ciné-Romans, he obtains an audition with Firmin Gémier who recommends him to Charles Dullin. Dullin offers him work with his workshop, the Atelier.

Late autumn: In Dullin's company he meets and falls in love with Genica Athanasiou (1897-1966).

1922   2 March: Plays King Galvan in Arnoux's *Moriano et Galvan* for which he also designed scenery and costumes.

20 June: Plays Basilio, King of Poland in Calderón's *Life is a Dream*, for which he also designed scenery and costumes.

July: Sees a troupe of Cambodian dancers, performing in a replica of the temple of Angkor at the Marseilles Colonial Exhibition.

October: Dullin's company moves into the theatre on the Place Dancourt on Montmartre which becomes the Théâtre de l'Atelier.

20 December: Artaud plays Tiresias in Cocteau's *Antigone* with Genica Athanasiou in the title role, sets by Picasso, costumes by Coco Chanel.

1923   Edits an anthology of Dr Toulouse's writings, *Au fil des préjugés*.

2 February: Publication of first number of Artaud's own literary periodical *Le Bilboquet*.

15 February: Appears in *Monsieur Pygmalion* by J. Grau in the part of a grotesque puppet at the Théâtre de l'Atelier.

April: Joins Pitoeff's troupe at the Comédie des Champs-Elysées.

1 May: start of the correspondence with Jacques Rivière (concluded 8 June 1924).

4 May: Artaud's first volume of poems *Tric-Trac du Ciel* published by Kahnweiler.

26 December: Plays Jackson in Andreyev's *He Who Gets Slapped* at the Comédie des Champs-Elysées.

1924   26 March: Plays a Robot in Capek's *RUR* under the direction of Theodore Kommissarjevsky at the Comédie des Champs-Elysées.

April: Films in Claude Autant-Lara's *Faits Divers*.

Summer: Films in Brittany in Luitz-Morat's *Surcouf*. Visits Berlin to work with UFA.

1 September: Publication of the correspondence with Jacques Rivière in the *Nouvelle Revue Française*.

7 September: Death of Artaud's father. His mother moves to Paris.

October: Joins the Surrealist movement.

1925   15 January: Contributes to No. 2 of *La Révolution Surréaliste*.

26 January: Becomes director of the Surrealists' Bureau de Recherches.

15 April: Appearance of No. 3 of *La Révolution Sur-réaliste*, edited and almost entirely written by Artaud.
28 and 29 May: *Au Pied du Mur* by Aragon, directed by Artaud at the Vieux Colombier.
3-11 June: Films in Marcel Vandal's *Graziella* on location in Italy (Procida, near Naples). Visits Pompeii and Rome.
23 July: *L'Ombilic des Limbes* published.
1 August: *Le Pèse-Nerfs* published.
Trips to Carteret (Manche) with Roger Vitrac.
August: Films in Luitz-Morat's *Le Juif Errant*.

1926   Foundation of the Théâtre Alfred Jarry (with Roger Vitrac and Robert Aron, and financial assistance from Madame Allendy).
November: *First Manifesto of the Théâtre Alfred Jarry* appears in the *Nouvelle Revue Française*.
End of November: Breaks with the Surrealists.

1927   Spring: Exchange of views with Jacques Maritain.
Films in Abel Gance's *Napoléon* in which he plays Marat.
1 and 2 June: First performances of the Théâtre Alfred Jarry at the Théâtre de Grenelle: Artaud's *Le Ventre Brûlé*; Max Robur's (i.e. Robert Aron's) *Gigogne*; and Vitrac's *Les Mystères de l'Amour*.
June: Carl Theodor Dreyer offers Artaud the part of the young monk in his film *La Passion de Jeanne d'Arc*.
Tries psychoanalytic treatment with Dr René Allendy.
October: Films in Léon Poirier's *Verdun, visions d'histoire*.
November: the *Nouvelle Revue Française* publishes Artaud's scenario for the film *La Coquille et le Clergyman*.
December: visits Cannes.

1928   14 January: Second production of the Théâtre Alfred Jarry at the Comédie des Champs-Elysées: Pudovkin's film *The Mother* and one act of Claudel's *Partage de Midi*.
18 February: First performance of *La Coquille et le Clergyman* (directed by Germaine Dulac) at the Studio des Ursulines. Artaud and Desnos create a disturbance to protest against the alleged misinterpretation of Artaud's intentions by the director.
22 March: Lectures at the Sorbonne on *L'Art et La Mort*.
2 and 9 June: Third production of the Théâtre Alfred Jarry: Strindberg's *Dream Play* at the Théâtre de l'Avenue. Disturbances caused by the Surrealists.

Films in Marcel Herbier's *L'Argent* (after Zola).

24 and 29 December: Fourth and last production of the Théâtre Alfred Jarry: *Victor* by Roger Vitrac at the Comédie des Champs-Elysées.

1929　5 January: Third performance of *Victor*.

February-April: Films in *Tarakanova*, directed by Raymond Bernard at the Nice studios.

26 April: Registers his adaptation of R. L. Stevenson's *The Master of Ballantrae* with the Association des Auteurs du Film.

17 April: *L'Art et La Mort* published by Denoel.

1930　July-August and October: Stays in Berlin to work on films, notably Pabst's version of Brecht's *Threepenny Opera*.

1931　January-March: Films in Raymond Bernard's *Faubourg Montmartre*.

Films in *La Femme de Nuit* (director; Marcel Herbier).

May: Films in *Les Croix de Bois* (directed by Raymond Bernard, based on Dorgelès's novel).

July: Sees Balinese Dancers perform at the Colonial Exhibition in the Bois de Vincennes.

End of liaison with Josette Lusson.

Publication of Artaud's free translation of *The Monk* by M. Lewis.

10 December: Lectures at the Sorbonne on *La Mise-en-scène et la métaphysique*.

1932　February: *La Mise-en-scène et la métaphysique* published by the *Nouvelle Revue Française*.

Project of a theatre sponsored by the *Nouvelle Revue Française*.

February-March: Assists Louis Jouvet in a production of Alfred Savoir's *La Patisserie du Village*.

April-May: in Berlin to film in *Coup de feu à l'aube* (directed by Serge de Poligny).

Adapts Seneca's *Thyestes*.

October: *First Manifesto of the Theatre of Cruelty*, published in the *Nouvelle Revue Française*.

December: In hospital for a disintoxication treatment.

1933　March: Beginning of friendship with Anais Nin.

April: Completes the manuscript of *Héliogabale*.

6 April: Lectures at the Sorbonne on *Le Théâtre et la Peste*. *Second Manifesto of the Theatre of Cruelty*.

Writes scenario for *La Conquête du Mexique*.

1934　6 January: Artaud reads *La Conquête du Mexique* and Shakespeare's *Richard II* at a soirée given by Lise Deharme at her home on the Quai Voltaire to raise funds for the Theatre of Cruelty.

Publication of *Héliogabale*.

Summer: On location in Algeria to film *Sidonie Panache* (directed by Henri Wullschleger).

Also acts in the following films: *Liliom* (directed by Fritz Lang); *Koenigsmarck* (directed by Marcel Tourneur); *Lucrèce Borgia* (directed by Abel Gance) in which he gives a memorable performance as Savonarola.

October: the *Nouvelle Revue Française* publishes 'Le Théâtre et la Peste'.

1935 February: Reads the manuscript of *Les Cenci* at the home of Jean-Marie Conty.

6 May: *Les Cenci* opens at the Folies-Wagram.

22 May: *Les Cenci* ends its run.

Autumn: Meets Cécile Schramme.

1936 9 January: Leaves Paris for Antwerp.

10 January: Sails from Antwerp on S.S. *Albertville*.

30 January: Arrives in Havana.

7 February: Disembarks at Veracruz.

April: Leaves Mexico City for the Sierra Tarahumara.

Beginning of October: Returns from the Sierra Tarahumara.

31 October: Leaves Mexico on S.S. *Mexique*.

12 November: Arrives at St Nazaire.

Writes *Les Nouvelles Révélations de l'Etre*.

Engagement to Cécile Schramme.

1937 March: Disintoxication treatment in Paris.

April: Renewed disintoxication cure at Sceaux.

May: Visit to Brussels.

18 May: Disastrous lecture at Brussels; the engagement to Cécile Schramme broken off.

28 July: *Les Nouvelles Révélations de l'Etre* published as an anonymous pamphlet.

1 August: *D'un voyage au pays des Tarahumaras* published anonymously in the *Nouvelle Revue Française*.

14 August: Arrives in Ireland at Cobh.

17 August: Leaves Galway for the Isles of Aran.

23 August: Writes from lodgings two hours walk from Kilronan, Isle of Inishmore.

2 September: At Imperial Hotel, Galway.

8 September: Leaves Galway for Dublin.

30 September: Arrives at Le Havre on S.S. *Washington*, under detention in a strait-jacket. Handed to French authorities.

1938 7 February: *Le Théâtre et son double* published.

12 April: Transferred to asylum of Sainte Anne, Paris.

December: At the Asylum of Quatre-Mares, Sotteville-lès-Rouen.

1939	27 February: Transferred to the asylum at Ville Evrard.
1943	22 January: Leaves asylum of Ville Evrard for temporary transfer to the 'rural' asylum at Chézal-Benoît.
	11 February: Arrives at the asylum of Rodez (Aveyron) and is put in the care of Dr Gaston Ferdière.
1944	10 May: Re-issue of *Le Théâtre et son double*.
1945	25 November: *Au pays des Tarahumaras* appears as a book.
1946	19 March: release from Rodez asylum for a short stay in the neighbourhood.
	8 April: *Lettres de Rodez* published by *GLM*.
	26 May: Returns to Paris. Takes up residence as a voluntary patient at Dr Delmas' mental hospital at Ivry.
	6 June: Opening of exhibition of works by leading painters donated to raise funds for Artaud, at the Galerie Pierre (director: Pierre Loeb).
	7 June: Benefit performance on Artaud's behalf at the Théâtre Sarah-Bernardt.
1947	13 January: Artaud appears at the Vieux Colombier in a series of poetry readings '*Tête-à-tête*'.
	January: Visits van Gogh Exhibition at the Orangerie.
	19 July: reads his own poetry at Galerie Pierre where an exhibition of his drawings is held.
	15 September: official publication date of *Artaud le Mômo* (the book actually available from 15 December).
	25 September: official publication date of *Van Gogh le suicidé de la société* (available in the shops ca 15 December).
	28 November: Recording of *Pour en finir avec le jugement de Dieu*.
	15 December: *Ci-gît* published (actually available from mid-January 1948).
1948	16 January: *Van Gogh* awarded the Prix St Beuve.
	2 February: Date for broadcast of *Pour en finir avec le jugement de Dieu*, cancelled the day before.
	5 February: *Pour en finir avec le jugement de Dieu* auditioned by a panel of distinguished literary figures who recommend that it should be transmitted.
	4 March: Artaud found dead in his room in the pavilion of the asylum at Ivry, 23, Rue de la Mairie, Ivry.
	8 March: Buried without religious rites at the cemetery of Ivry.

Bibliography

1. ARTAUD'S WRITINGS

The collected edition of Artaud's works and letters is:

Artaud, Antonin, *Oeuvres Complétes*, Paris, Gallimard, 1956–
Of this fourteen volumes had appeared by the end of 1957,
i.e. volumes I-XIII and a supplementary volume to volume I.
Volumes I-II originally published in 1956 and 1961 have been
re-issued in a revised and augmented form as volume I, 1970.
Supplément au tome I, 1970, volume II, 1973.

In the spring of 1976 a further revised version of volume I and
its supplement appeared in two half-volumes, with the announce-
ments that they were the first in a new revised edition of
the *Oeuvres Complètes* which would include new material
discovered since the first series was started.

There is a further volume of letters:
Artaud, Antonin, *Lettres à Genica Athanasiou*. Paris, Gallimard,
1969.

The fullest bibliography of Artaud's writings scattered in
pamphlets and periodicals can be found in Alain Virmaux's
book listed below.

2. TRANSLATIONS
An English translation of Artaud's collected works is appearing
in London:
Artaud, Antonin, *Collected Works*, translated by Victor Corti.
London, Calder & Boyars, 1968–
Of this four volumes had appeared by the end of 1975.

In the United States *The Theatre and its Double* is available
in a translation by C. Richards, published by Grove Press,
New York, 1958.

An excellent selection of Artaud's poems and late essays is:

Hirschman, Jack (ed.), *Antonin Artaud Anthology*. San Francisco, City Lights Books, 1965.

3. SPECIAL NUMBERS OF PERIODICALS DEVOTED TO ARTAUD

Cahiers de la Compagnie Renaud-Barrault, No. 22-23, May 1958
La Tour de Feu, Jarnac (Charente) No. 63/64, December 1959
La Tour de Feu, No. 69, April 1961
La Tour de Feu, No. 112, December 1971
Tulane Drama Review, No. 22, Winter 1963
Tel Quel, No. 20, Winter 1965
Tel Quel, No. 52, Winter 1972

4. BOOKS ABOUT ARTAUD

Armand-Laroche, Dr. J.-L., *Antonin Artaud et son Double*. Périgueux, Pierre Fanlac, 1964
Barrault, Jean-Louis, *Souvenirs pour demain*. Paris, Editions du Seuil, 1972
Blanchot, Maurice, *Le livre à venir*. Paris, Gallimard, 1959
Brau, Jean-Louis, *Antonin Artaud*. Paris, La Table Ronde, 1971
Bugard, Pierre, *Le Comédien et son double*. Paris, Stock, 1970
Charbonnier, Georges, *Essai sur Antoine Artaud*. Paris, Eeghers, 1959
Deleuze, Gilles and Guattari, Félix, *L'Anti-Oedipe*. Paris, Editions de Minuit, 1972
Derrida, Jacques, *L'Ecriture et la différence*. Paris, Editions du Seuil, 1967
Durozoi, Gérard, *Artaud: l'aliénation et la folie*. Paris, Larousse, 1972
Foucault, Michel, *Histoire de la folie*. Paris, Plon, 1961
Gouhier, Henri, *Antonin Artaud et l'essence du théâtre*. Paris, Vrin, 1974
Greene, Naomi, *Antonin Artaud: Poet without Words*. New York, Simon and Schuster, 1970
Hahn, Otto, *Portrait d'Antonin Artaud*, Paris. Soleil Noir, 1968
Hort, Jean, *Antonin Artaud, le suicidé de la société*. Geneva, Editions Connaître, 1960
Knapp, Bettina L., *Antonin Artaud, Man of Vision*. New York, Discus Books, 1971
Matthews, J. H., *Theatre in Dada and Surrealism*. Syracuse, Syracuse University Press, 1974
Nin, Anais, *The Journals of Anais Nin*. 5 vols, London, Peter Owen, 1966-1974
Prevel, Jacques, *En compagnie d'Antonin Artaud*. Paris, Flammarion, 1974

Sellin, Eric, *The Dramatic Concepts of Antonin Artaud*. Chicago, University of Chicago Press, 1968

Sollers, Philippe, (ed.), *Artaud*. Paris, 10/18, 1973

Sontag, Susan, 'Approaching Artaud'. *New Yorker*, May 19, 1973.

Tonnelli, Franco, *L'Esthétique de la Cruauté*. Paris, Nizet, 1972

Virmaux, Alain, *Antonin Artaud et le théâtre*, Paris, Seghers, 1970

Beckett

A. Alvarez

Samuel Beckett's reputation as a master of modern literature is established beyond doubt and widely recognized, and yet his work is at once allusive and highly concentrated, as well as original in form, approach, and theme. The whole world of feeling which Lawrence and other modern writers take to be the one certain good, is for Beckett no more than a guarantee of suffering. Hence the need for a book which, like this one, provides a guide to Beckett's work that is as clear and full as their difficulty requires without losing touch with their strangeness.

'As a non-specialist's introductory guide to Beckett's work, this book has considerable merit. It is much more readable than almost anything of its kind to date.' *The Irish Press*

'This is an excellent addition to the Modern Master series, and also one of the best things written about Beckett. Mr Alvarez writes a cool, lucid prose and his critical stance is scrupulous and watchful. He distinguishes acutely between Beckett's finest and lesser achievements and conveys the imaginative and intellectual complexities of his work without overloading his own prose.' *The Sunday Times*